AFFILIATE MARKETING SECRETS

For 2019 and Beyond

A Comprehensive Guide to Master the Online Affiliate Marketing World

By

Brett Smith

First Edition 2018

Copyright – Brett Smith

All rights reserved.

No part of this publication may be reproduced, stored in or introduced into a retrieval system, or transmitted in any form, or by any means (electronic, mechanical, photocopying, recording or otherwise) without the prior written permission of the author.

This book is sold subject to the condition that is shall not, by way of trade or otherwise, be lent, resold, hired out or otherwise circulated without the author's prior consent in any form of binding or cover other than that in which it is published and without a similar condition including this condition being imposed on the subsequent purchaser.

A note from the author…

Welcome to "Affiliate Marketing Secrets".

This book contains a comprehensive and an extensive guide with the latest strategies to master the evolving online affiliate marketing world in the year 2019 and beyond.

The internet is constantly changing. Therefore, all internet based businesses need to be evolving with up to date marketing and business strategies in order to sustain long term.

This book covers all you need to know in order to be successful in the evolving internet world not only as a beginner to affiliate marketing, but also as an experienced online entrepreneur.

However, keep in mind that just by reading this book, money is not going to fall from the sky through the roof on to your table. To be successful financially, work is always required. No one is successful at anything in the world without taking action and putting in the work that is required.

In order to get the maximum value out of this book, get a pen and a notebook alongside with you. Turn on your computer and get prepared. Whenever you get a new idea, jot it down and implement it right away. Speed of implantation equals speed of success.

The strategies included in this book helped me and my students to create successful affiliate marketing businesses, and predicted by super experienced professionals that they are the best to work with in the future.

We have created our financial freedom by being successful at making money online. Now it is time for you!

Introduction

Imagine that you could earn commissions for sales on a popular brand-name product just by placing a link on your website or in your email, and sending buyers through it. That simply is "Affiliate Marketing"!

The process is not quite that simple, but it does not have to be much more complicated either.

To begin with a few definitions, an advertiser, or merchant, is the company who is selling a product. An affiliate, sometimes referred to as a publisher or partner, is another person or company who assists in the promotion of the product and earns a commission for doing so, every time when a sale is made. In between is the account management service that collaborates the advertisers with the affiliates and keeps track of the sales and commissions.

The numerous benefits of affiliate marketing include the potential for profiting. You can robotize a great deal of the promoting procedure and get installment just for wanted outcomes, which incorporates deals, enlistments, and snaps.

Despite the fact that most dealers will expect some level of hazard with misrepresentation, there is yet a level of hazard included. When you realize what you are doing with affiliate marketing, you will be on top well previously you know it.

Affiliate marketing has been a contributor to the ascent of numerous organizations web based, including Amazon.com. Amazon.com was one of the principal adopters of affiliate marketing, and now has a large number of affiliate connections. Concerning profiting, affiliate marketing is in its very own group. You do not need to stress over managers breathing down your neck, and you are responsible for all that you do with your organization and your site.

Affiliate marketing likewise allows you to remain behind items you know and love, be offering connections and flags to them on your own site. You will get cash for every item bought that you speak to, or, in other words enough to take part. If you have been searching for additional cash, affiliate marketing is the best approach. You can stay with one shipper or run with the same number of as you requirement for your business. Affiliate marketing on the web is genuinely ending up increasingly famous - making presently the ideal opportunity for you to get your foot in the entryway.

Table of Contents

1: **Stepping in to the Affiliate World in 2019 and Beyond** …07

2: **Making Money Online in the Future** …21

3: **The Niche Selection Game Plan** …31

4: **Conversion Strategies** …49

5: **Google and Fast Traffic Secrets** …67

6: **SEO and Other Powerful Income Boosting Tools** …86

7: **Affiliate Marketing Future Trends and Success Guidelines**

…107

8: **The Gift Package** …191

Downloadable links of:

- 12-Step Video Course on How to Build Your Own Online PLR Business
- 1,000 Ebooks with Private Label Rights
- 100,000 Articles with Private Label Rights

Chapter 1

Stepping in to the Affiliate World in 2019 and Beyond

Being an affiliate includes offering items for other individuals and making a commission off that item. These items can run from digital books to cleanser to grown-up toys. Most affiliates offer multivitamins and other basic items that everything except offer themselves. These projects are endorsed by bigger organizations that need to offer their items in a less customary way.

All together for the person to profit on the affiliate projects, he or she must be a businessperson and there must a drive. There are numerous individuals who will state that affiliate programs are basic cash, but these people are more than likely making their deals in untrustworthy strategies. Through diligent work, individuals can get away from the limits of conventional work and turn into their very own supervisor and run their own store. This requires some serious energy, it takes commitment and it takes work.

The affiliate program can get less demanding as the individual takes part in it. This is on account of once the program is available and individuals end up mindful of it, they will probably focus on it. There will be return clients and they will spread the news about the program to those that they know and these individuals will purchase the items that the affiliate offers to them. These fulfilled clients at that point thus spread more word about the items.

The affiliate program regularly takes some start up cash in the first place. While the expression "You don't burn through cash to profit" is normally valid, in the affiliate program this isn't the situation. Usually important to construct some stock and have test items for individuals to attempt before they make a buy (particularly when you are offering items disconnected).

There is a science to being an affiliate. This science includes finding an affiliate program which pays well and which offers a practical item. From that point, you should choose how best to showcase that item. Monitoring the wage and the deals is likewise imperative for assessment purposes. The majority of this can represent the moment of truth a man who needs to begin his or her own independent company utilizing existing affiliate programs. By focusing on the rules clarified here, you can boost your odds of doing great as an affiliate.

Finding A Product

The vast majority would accept that finding the item to offer as an affiliate would be the simple part. This isn't generally the situation, however. There are a huge number of different items on the Internet that are great decisions for an affiliate to offer. Not these items are beneficial and not every gainful item merit offering as an affiliate.

When contemplating an item to offer as an affiliate, consider first the items you have by and by tried and appreciated (or for which you have great proof that they are high caliber).

This is the way toward discovering items you really have faith in and can bolster. This will guarantee that the item is of good quality and something that individuals really need. What's more, if the item is something that somebody trusts in, it makes it simpler to offer.

There are many affiliate programs that can be discovered on the web. Choosing which one to utilize involves inclination and confidence in the item. Every one of these different projects will have different commission rates for deals and different beginning expenses.

A standout amongst other approaches to locate the correct affiliate program is to utilize an affiliate index site. A standout amongst other affiliate catalogs on the Internet is the site http://www.AffiliatePrograms.com. Other great choices including http://www.commissionjunction.com and http://www.clickbank.com. These locales give the data about a wide range of kinds of affiliate programs, including commission rates and item prevalence. There are programs for retail items the distance to travel and site administrations. The projects are recorded in sequential order arrange on the first page and they are arranged by class.

To utilize this site, just tap on kind of affiliate program that one is keen on beginning and after that read the data about the affiliate program itself. This data is refreshed frequently. To pick an affiliate program, essentially tap on the title of the fascinating project and it will take you to the site. This will at that point enable you to acquire an affiliate ID and relating affiliate joins, which you can use to offer the item.

Another approach to locate the correct affiliate program is to go to "parties" where an item is being sold. If the individual finds an item that he or she enjoys and needs to offer, approach the merchant and talk about turning into an affiliate. The most well-known gatherings incorporate satchel parties, gems gatherings, and make up gatherings. The greater part of these gatherings are controlled by ladies, in spite of the fact that men are allowed to wind up affiliates too. Avon, Mary Kay, and Pampered Chef are the most widely recognized gatherings that individuals encounter.

What To Look For When Promoting a Product

• You will need to search for a program that is of high caliber. For example, search for one that is related with numerous specialists in that specific industry. Along these lines, you can be guaranteed of the standard of the program you will join.

• Look for the ones that offer genuine and practical items. How would you know this? Do some underlying examination. If conceivable, find a portion of the individuals and clients to give you tribute on the believability of the program.

• Does the program oblige a developing target showcase? This will guarantee you that there will be a persistent interest for your referrals. Complete a little research and make request. If there are gatherings and exchanges bunches identified with the item subject take part and search for dependable input.

- A program with a remuneration plan that pays out a leftover pay and a payout of at least 30% would be an extraordinary decision.

- There are programs offering this sort of remuneration. You simply need to look carefully for one. Try not to squander your time with projects that don't remunerate generously for your endeavors.

- Be mindful of any base quantities that you should satisfy. Some affiliate programs force pre-necessities before you get your bonuses. For example you may need to make in excess of a $100.00 or influence ten deals previously you to get your paycheck. If the business target is too difficult to accomplish you might need to reexamine joining.

- Select programs that have a lot of pre made apparatuses and assets that can enable you to develop the business in the briefest conceivable time. Not all affiliate programs have these limits.

- Check out climate or not the program has a mechanized framework that enables you to check your referral measurements and pay whenever.

- Does the program offer solid motivations for clients to make extra buys or for individuals to recharge their participations. Affiliate programs that give persistent help and moves up to its items tend to hold more clients. These things can guarantee the development of your business.

Marketing A Product

Indeed, even the best items available need some publicizing. Without publicizing and marketing, people in general won't realize that the item exists. What is much more essential for an affiliate program is the publicizing of the program and the store. This mix of publicizing an item and the store will draw more individuals onto the business floor and this will result in more deals.

There are no set standards for how to showcase an item. Rather there are recommendations that can enable a man to showcase the item, the store, and themselves. This can result in more deals and in this way more cash. These techniques are not free, but rather the final product can without much of a stretch pay for the cash that is put into the marketing procedure.

Now and again, it may be best to enlist an expert through a site like http://www.elance.com to discover capable individuals who can showcase the item you're advancing.

Article marketing is an incredible type of free movement to advertise any item, including affiliate items. All you require is a 350-500 word article composed and submit it to article indexes like goarticles.com, articlecity.com and some more. There are truly many articles destinations you can distribute your article to. You'll pick up bunches of presentation along these lines. If you're not a major devotee of thinking of, you can contract journalists to compose articles for you. Many independent destinations like elance.com and guru.com offer these administrations.

Site Use

More individuals shop online now than any time in recent memory. There are numerous stores that have shut their physical retail facades and now work just on the web. There are a ton of reasons why sites have a tendency to improve the situation than customary stores. The most practical reason is that the costs can be kept lower in light of the fact that there is less overhead. The block customer facing facade requires the individual to really lease a place for a few hundred every month, procure a representative to man the store, pay utilities and protection and different expenses of business. The best way to cover these costs is to energize a significant stamp on the items sold in the store.

Web based organizations have a much lower overhead than the customary store. A site is shoddy, and at times free, to have. Most sites are close to $50 dollars multi month to have. Sites like VistaPrint.com even take into consideration free site facilitating for multi month and after that shabby month to month costs. Different locales like Weebly.com offer free site facilitating for a weebly.com site and low expenses for a genuine .com space name.

These sites don't should be worked by a creator. These sites are simple for anybody with minor PC aptitudes to construct and most have well ordered bearings. They are straightforward point and snap sites that offer client benefit delegates if the individual building the site stalls out. For the individuals who need an exceptionally expert and emerge site, these organizations offer to have the destinations worked by an expert for a set charge. The accomplishment of the site is then ensured.

Simply having a site isn't sufficient marketing to do with the end goal to guarantee that individuals see the site. The site should be publicized and it should be streamlined for site improvement. This should be possible by including a blog and always refreshing its substance. Moreover, you should seriously mull over labeling specific inquiry words and by running AdWords battles to publicize the site.

Pictures and recordings are likewise enormous draws for the sites and can create movement to the site. The more activity the site gets, the better the odds of a man making a buy from the site. It is a smart thought to offer a great deal of pictures and a few recordings of the affiliate getting surveys or informing individuals regarding the items offered on the site. This can build the draw extensively and guarantee that the general population who achieve the site are taught on the items themselves.

It is critical to recall that in light of the fact that the affiliate is a decent salesman and that he might be equipped for building a site, he may require help making sites or duplicate compose material for promoting purposes. Website design enhancement, or site improvement can likewise be exceptionally difficult and he may require help. It is best that he utilizes an expert composition, for example, the ones on Elance.com- - to guarantee that the composition and substance is proficient and viable for publicizing purposes.

Store Displays

Another smart thought is to converse with the private companies and stores in the nearby region about facilitating the items on their racks. This works by pitching the items at a marked down cost to the store and enabling them to offer the items at a the maximum. This gives the items to an open that likes to shop at a customary store as opposed to an online one.

This likewise diminishes the overhead in light of the fact that the store proprietor would take care of the expenses of promoting for the item. He or she would likewise be taking care of the expenses related with running a block store, including the individual expected to run the store. This can mean more benefits for the affiliate despite the fact that the items were sold at a less expensive rate than ordinary. It is critical to utilize this reduced rate for the store since the store will purchase more items and the store will likewise need to make a benefit generally the store will suspend the item on their racks.

When moving toward a store about facilitating a showcase about your item recall that a few stores really have mother stores that don't permit this. Regardless of whether the store proprietor gets discourteous, don't pursue suite. Rather, smoothly say thanks to them for their time and leave. Continuously be an expert. Another smart thought is to convey a little example of the items into the store. This will pitch the item to the store proprietor.

If the store proprietor enables the affiliate to set up a showcase, make certain not to make it too huge or excessively unpleasant. By having a littler and expert looking presentation, the store proprietor will probably enable it to stay set up and individuals will give careful consideration to something that does not hurt their eyes to view.

If the store proprietor enables the item to be shown on the racks with alternate items, join put cards to the rack that depict what the item is furthermore, why it is so powerful. This will instruct general society and it will drive deals. This is for the affiliate's and the store proprietor's advantage if the general population is more inspired by the items.

Informal exchange

Informal exchange is a standout amongst the best promoting strategies out there. This is can work both ways however, and this is the reason it is so imperative to give an item that is of high caliber instead of one that is modest and does not perform. Verbal exchange is free publicizing and it achieves a large number of individuals consistently, one individual at any given moment.

The vast majority discuss items that they appreciate and that they like. The better the item, the more individuals will discuss utilizing it. They will express that it is so natural to utilize, how moderate it is, the quality and why their companions should all get one. The verbal exchange is regularly more acknowledged by a more extensive number of individuals than some other methods for correspondence about an item.

The drawback to informal exchange is that if individuals don't care for the item, they will be clear about this too. This is the reason it is imperative to just offer items that are high caliber and worth the cash that the general population are putting down for it. Presently, there will dependably be those people who feel that they didn't get their cash out of an item. There is no assistance for this, but if the level of these individuals is low, at that point the verbal ad technique can be exceptionally powerful.

Verbal exchange can likewise be utilized on the site through a procedure called looking into. These surveys are individuals' confirmations with respect to how the item functioned for them. There are a few sites that will create tributes, but these are exploitative sites and individuals are frequently ready to tell if the declaration is false or valid by the manner in which it is worded and composed. Everybody has a novel composition style, and attempting to make counterfeit declarations implies that the different clients will have a similar tone and composing style.

Verbal exchange is viewed as an aloof publicizing technique since it isn't really done by the affiliate. The affiliate essentially kicks back and sits tight for the clients to enlighten their companions and neighbors regarding the item, bringing about new deals and new clients. This ought not be the main methods for publicizing that the affiliate uses to push deals. It is problematic.

Promoting

There are different techniques for publicizing that ought to be made reference to as they are to a great degree viable, albeit more conventional. The first is flyer ads. The second is business card ads. Announcement and mass travel ad is additionally accessible for utilize.

These strategies for publicizing help to enable the general population to see the promoting in a genuine setting. The flyers can be sent specifically to their letter drop and they can instruct and intrigue people in general to visiting the store or site where the items are sold. The business card commercials are comparable but they are left those regions where there is a great deal of activity and they are regularly found by potential clients who have their advantage topped by seeing the card. Both of these strategies can be taken care of by marketing locales, for example, VistaPrint.com.

Bulletins and mass travel promoting are both genuinely costly methods of publicizing, despite the fact that they do strike many individuals. These strategies have the drawback of not having the capacity to be found in the home where the general population approach the web. This implies individuals may not really follow up on the promoting that they see, regardless of being instantly intrigued by it.

TV and radio promotions are likewise customary techniques for publicizing. Lamentably, these strategies have a tendency to be extremely costly. It is prescribed that affiliates don't utilize this technique except if they are now encountering achievement and can manage the cost of the cost. This can be extremely viable as more individuals are utilizing the PC as they stare at the TV or tune in to the radio.

Internet promoting is an obviously better methodology of publicizing since it's shoddy and simple to setup. You can begin utilizing pay-per-click administrations like Google AdWords to publicize rapidly and effectively. You just pay at whatever point somebody clicks on your ad.

Monitoring Sales

As far as following on the web affiliate deals, most vendors like Clickbank.com have their own worked in deals measurements so you can perceive what number of offers you made, who purchased what et cetera. When you agree to accept affiliate programs, you're regularly given points of interest on where and how to login to check your details. This would be an extraordinary asset to track your deals.

It's dependably a smart thought to know your measurements with the goal that you know if your endeavors are giving the outcomes you need. Your measurements are your transformation rates. What number of individuals tapped on your connection? Our of those individuals who clicked, what number of purchased the item? Where did the source originate from? These are critical points of interest you should know.

Beginning a business that offers affiliate items can be exceptionally energizing and extremely beneficial— regardless of whether you offer fundamentally disconnected items or basically electronic items. Be that as it may, the procedure isn't as straightforward as joining and viewing the cash come in. There is a considerable measure that should be done with the end goal to guarantee that the items achieve the clients, that the item is found by clients and that the fundamental assessment data is kept up. Each part of maintaining this business requires the abilities and consideration of the affiliate person.

If pondering joining an affiliate program, converse with other people who are as of now individuals from that affiliate program. See what they are doing and how they are getting along. Decide whether others are effective in the program and discover a strategy for success that works best for one's specific needs, monetarily and time shrewd. This can enhance the fulfillment of being an affiliate part and one's general happiness regarding life.

Utilizing the affiliate programs, one can genuinely turn into his or her very own manager. It is just however the right and committed utilization of the marketing program this can really happen and individuals can appreciate the life that is then advertised. When the underlying leg work is done, it tends to be conceivable to make a huge number of dollars multi month utilizing the affiliate programs like they promote. Appreciate it, buckle down at it, and it will satisfy.

Chapter 2

Making Money Online in the Future

Who knows what amount of cash is made on the web every single day? If you could put a figure on it around the world, would it be billions? More? Crosswise over countries and monetary forms that would be difficult to make sense of. But we do realize that cash is made continuously on the web; we additionally realize that a significant number of the general population making that cash are tranquil people sitting in the solace of their own homes. Many are not by any stretch of the imagination working at all at the specific same time their cash is being made. Affiliate advertisers are barely ever around while their sites continue profiting.

The web is one of the most effortless approaches to profit, especially if you need to profit from your home, or profit in a way that costs close to nothing and profits many-crease for your speculation of little or nothing. It has permitted individuals from all kinds of different backgrounds to profit—huge cash—and quit their day employments (or as a rule, never begin one in the first place). Furthermore, shockingly, profiting on the web does not require the kind of foundation, instruction, or experience that the vast majority figure it does. Profiting on the web has been made progressively less demanding, opening the entryway for an ever increasing number of individuals to sit back, unwind, and let the ethereal World Wide Web profit for them.

So by what means can a man or lady—with or without a working learning of PC programming or business—profit on the web? What's more, by what means can he or she do as such without enduring the screen of a PC for quite a long time and days on end?

For an extremely entrenched number of individuals and a regularly developing populace of web clients, the appropriate response is web marketing, all the more specifically known as affiliate marketing. But as the name may be taken to infer, affiliate marketing does not require a promoting degree, or even a comprehension of the codes and projects that run the web. With the devices and assets accessible, any individual who can peruse or can type (and not well, we may include) can be an online affiliate, and can supplant his or her pay with the wage produced as what we call a Big Shot Affiliate.

What is a Big Shot Affiliate?

A Big Shot Affiliate is one who shows improvement over the rest. While any possibility little affiliates may make a couple of bucks all over, the Big Shots profit (six figures isn't at all phenomenal) on a predictable premise. They construct their affiliate organizations with one aim—to profit effectively, and to live the manner in which it ought to be lived, in solace and in simplicity.

What separates the Big Shots is the accomplishment of their affiliate organizations. But what truly separates them is knowing the traps, tips, and apparatuses of the exchange that make it feasible for customary folks and young ladies to become wildly successful. That is exactly what this book was composed for—to demonstrate you, regardless of your identity, how you can prevail as an online affiliate, and how you, as well, can enter the positions of the Big Shot affiliates and accomplish more than make some additional money to stroll around with. We've placed everything into this book you should be different; all that you should be the person who brings home the bacon as an affiliate, not an additional wage. All that you should be a Big Shot.

Should it truly be possible?

The main inquiry that strikes a chord for individuals contemplating profiting with easy revenue from affiliate organizations and web marketing is this: Can it truly be finished?

The short answer—yes. It can. It is. It is done each day. Consistently, the Big Shot Affiliates are making huge cash doing practically nothing. Saying this doesn't imply that they never place work in ever. The Big Shots absolutely do. But once the greater part of the work is done, the Big Shots go to play and let the web do their work for them.

This conveys us to the principal point—there is work engaged with profiting as an affiliate. But isn't that precisely in opposition to the point of being an affiliate advertiser? Not by any stretch of the imagination. The key is knowing how to function more quick witted, not harder, and establishing the framework that will profit while you play, get-away, lie in the sun, rest, or even work somewhere else if you truly need to.

To return to the current inquiry, and to clarify that inquiry, yes individuals do make cash as affiliates. But they don't make cash by doing nothing. The general population who make cash as affiliates begin with an arrangement. They explore what it takes to wind up a fruitful affiliate and online advertiser (much in the manner in which you are doing well at this point). They find out about the devices accessible to them, and about the assets and items that believer to deals—to affiliate wage. And after that they go to work.

What makes Big Shot Affiliates different?

The one factor that isolates the Big Shots from the rest—the general population profiting with affiliate projects, or who never observe any wage as affiliates whatsoever—is constancy. While it is conceivable to begin seeing a decent leftover wage in brief time, it isn't exceptionally reasonable to make a whole living off it that rapidly. It requires investment to get results as an affiliate, and requires exertion to set up every one of the pieces so your affiliate program can begin profiting without you there. When that is done, you unquestionably can be a Big Shot profiting for just a couple of long periods of work all over.

A great many people bomb as affiliates since they complete one of two things wrong; either,

- They don't do any work to begin with, or

- They don't give it enough time

But if you are eager, capable, and arranged to put in some work first and foremost, and willing to stick it out, you will have the capacity to supplant your salary, or to construct your wage, and you will have the capacity to support that pay on only a couple of long stretches of work.

For what reason would it be advisable for you to think about it?

Since you know there are individuals out there making cash as affiliates, you may inquire as to why you by and by ought to think about turning into an affiliate, and why you should put the time, cash, and exertion into being a Big Shot affiliate advertiser.

Cash

We'll begin with the most disposable reason—cash. Why put your well deserved money into building a business as a web advertiser? Simply, in light of the fact that building an affiliate business is one of indisputably the slightest costly organizations you could be in. Actually, it doesn't need to cost you anything by any stretch of the imagination. Being an affiliate is free. You should simply join or enlist with the item supplier and you're in!

But shouldn't something be said about sites and facilitating costs? Those can be had for nothing also. What's more, should you move up to a more adaptable and higher quality site, you can do that for almost no cash (and this you should do). Regardless of whether you're not a software engineer, or know nothing at all about making sites, coding, and everything off camera of site building, you can have a site with easy to understand (read, no innovative aptitude required) layouts for less than ten dollars for every month. That is no lie. These locales are out there. Two or three well known ones that strike a chord are GoDaddy.com and HostGator.com, but there are numerous others, and numerous newcomers hoping to serve this sought after market, as well (some that are notwithstanding facilitating affiliate programs!).

Time

Individuals presumably grumble most about an absence of cash when beginning another business; absence of time is the following most regular grievance that would-be Big Shot affiliates use to reason against resolving to affiliate organizations. You simply don't have room schedule-wise to commit to beginning a business starting with no outside help. Well perhaps not if you're re-imagining the wheel, but rather affiliate marketing doesn't work that way.

There are a heap of instruments accessible for affiliates. Know the instruments to utilize that will enable you to profit, and you extremely decrease the measure of time expected to get your new pursuit up and running. But we lose track of the main issue at hand. Since the point additionally is that the organizations who need you to be their affiliates have done a large portion of the work for you. They've composed the promotions, created the code, planned the designs, and as a rule assembled finish affiliate sites. You should simply discover some place to have them with the goal that individuals can discover your connections and navigate to purchase from your advertisements so you get a level of those deals. You should simply put the correct item at the perfect place at the opportune time. Of course, there are approaches to do this with the goal that deals are made, and that is truly what this book is about. But rest guaranteed that you can make an opportunity to manufacture a fruitful affiliate business. You can do it a hour on end or days on end. Whatever time you can distribute is time that will bring you wage through affiliate deals.

Exertion

We won't mess with you. You do need to invest some exertion with the end goal to appreciate income sans work through web deals. You won't invest as much exertion, say, as the person who is hand-weaving natural fleece covers and afterward endeavoring to offer them on the web, but you should put some genuine, centered exertion into being an affiliate—at first.

A great part of the time and exertion that is required is just in the first place. Once you've constructed your stage and took in the nuts and bolts, you require just to keep up. So it might take twenty hours of strong work (a hour on end or multi day on end) to get you there, but then you should simply keep up. Once you've hit the level of upkeep, that is the place you can truly unwind. Sit back, have a good time, and be sluggish like the Big Shots. Devote a couple of hours seven days to keeping up the wage stream and activity that you've picked up, and money your affiliate remarkably coming in.

Adaptability

What does each pooch need from life? The opportunity to have a decent time. What is opportunity? Today, opportunity is typically having the adaptability to run your activity around your life, not have your life circled your activity. That is something you unquestionably can do as a Big Shot affiliate. There's no more noteworthy level of adaptability than a business that runs itself. What's more, that is the magnificence of the web. It's the reason everybody needs to be in an e-business. Since it's never off, and the potential for income are dependably on; and you can take care of it when you need, not when a manager or a customer requests.

Pay Potential

The pay capability of affiliate marketing is for all intents and purposes boundless. The additional time, exertion, and assets you need to put into it, the more cash you can make with it. But even better, you can profit without a lot of that. For what other reason be around here? Is it safe to say that it isn't about the pain free income? The enormous undercut and huge checks for quite a long time? It surely is. When you figure out how the Big Shots do it, you can be making the greater, better, simpler bucks, as well. And afterward if you're feeling vigorous, you can go for additional. That likewise requires knowing the correct devices and right items that you by and by can use to profit on the web. That requires perusing whatever is left of this book and discovering what those are.

To whole it up, you ought to consider affiliate marketing therefore:

- Affiliate marketing is an ease (perhaps no-cost) business to be in

- Affiliate marketing requires restricted exertion, taking up constrained measures of your time

- With the adaptability of affiliate business, you're in charge

- For your constrained time, cash, and exertion, you can make boundless pay

Would we be able to give you more reasons? Most likely, but you get the drift, so how about we get on to more imperative things.

Examples of overcoming adversity

As though our reason weren't adequate, we'll entice you with an outline of affiliate examples of overcoming adversity. These accounts flourish on the web. You can discover them anyplace. They originate from individuals youthful and old.

Frequently the old are the individuals who got in when the getting was great and consummated the craft of affiliate marketing. These are the general population who invented the affiliate wheel, the specialists you are gaining from today—the first Big Shots.

The youthful that we see are those sufficiently brilliant to realize that there is pain free income to be made on the web. They were brought up in a PC culture, and knew from at an opportune time that there was no purpose behind them to buckle down and ache for their cash the manner in which their folks did. So they didn't.

We see folks like Jason Calacanis making upwards of $3,000 every day with basic projects like Google AdSense, which your seven-year-old could enable you to utilize; or the folks and young ladies making a more than open to living by utilizing affiliate apparatuses like Commission Junction, or with huge name affiliates like eBay. And after that we see the general population who aren't utilizing huge name relationship by any stretch of the imagination, that are simply marketing the little, but truly necessary projects individuals are scanning for.

They do it on sites and web journals, on discussions and in messages. They do it for all intents and purposes wherever on the web, and they do profit. We won't bore you here with names of individuals you have no enthusiasm for knowing, but we can let you know unequivocally that these individuals are out there. Google 'affiliate examples of overcoming adversity's and you'll have more than the evidence you require.

Chapter 3

The Niche Selection Game Plan

Exposing the Myths about Niche Selection

One of unquestionably the most prolific recommendations for planned affiliates is to work inside their interests—to discover their specialty advertise in a zone of individual intrigue and remain with it. While there is a place for specialty marketing in affiliate marketing, it isn't what you have been persuaded that it is. Without a doubt, "work inside your own specialty" is one of the most noticeably bad suggestions given to new business visionaries, and the reason for huge numbers of affiliate disappointments.

Do what intrigues you

Do what intrigues you; discover your specialty; do what you are energetic about; offer the items that intrigue you the most...

These are the suggestions that business visionaries are read a clock and once more. Furthermore, there is some premise to this idea, some technique behind this frenzy.

The general conviction is that if you work together in a region or 'specialty' that you are profoundly inspired by, that energy will radiate through and you will make deals inadvertently. The inclination is that by offering items or working inside your most loved specialty you will have a worked in feeling of criticalness and want that will constrain you to take a shot at your business and to succeed.

In addition, by working inside a specialty class of individual intrigue you will come arranged. That is, you will come furnished with pail heaps of learning and encounters with different items so you don't need to 'sit idle' getting up to speed. You'll definitely know the items that merit advancement. What's more, you'll know all the limited time foundation data relatively off the highest point of your head.

The conviction is that if you center around advancing items that are somehow important to you, you can without much of a stretch do what needs to be done. You can develop sites that will offer the items; you can compose articles to submit to indexes and restore connections to you, the specialty master; you can construct blog upon blog and never come up short on something extraordinary to say in regards to your most loved little gadget that so changed your life as a gadget authority (regardless of whether you ought to or not, is another issue, and we'll talk about that later).

Here's the thing about this—none of it is false. It is less demanding to put yourself behind an item you definitely know. It is less demanding to get down to business when you are now knowledgeable in issues. It is less demanding to associate with guests and perusers who are more similar to you.

So why, at that point, is it a legend to trust that you should concentrate first and premier on your own advantage specialty as an affiliate advertisers? For what reason can't that mean for all intents and purposes programmed deals and commissions?

What's off with enthusiasm?

The thinking against individual specialty focus is more oversimplified than you may might suspect. Also, in purpose of actuality, there are a few special cases to the standard, which we can contact upon after you comprehend why the fantasy by and large is a legend.

At that point quit wasting time officially, isn't that so? What's the issue with accomplishing something you are energetic about?

There is nothing genuinely amiss with it. But there is something unbeneficial about it in an overwhelmingly expansive level of cases. What is unfruitful about this attitude is that it is simply excessively constraining. By picking your business and items dependent on one individual inclination, you lose the opportunity of decision. Furthermore, that opportunity is essential, since it is the thing that enables you to give purchasers what they need, and seats you with a predetermined number of affiliate item alternatives, more often than not in a specialty that isn't seeing popularity.

Simply, except if your specialty premium happens to be in items or branches of knowledge that harmonize with what individuals are prepared to get, it doesn't accompany the most fundamental component of affiliate marketing achievement—worked in clients.

Rather than concentrating on the specialty items, you have to center around the items that can and do offer. In any event if you need to be one of the Big Shots in web marketing you do. If you need to make the enormous commission checks and the simple, offer themselves-while-I'm-in-the-tropics sort of offers the Big Shots do, you need to ponder what you need to discuss and more about what clients need to hear.

The other factor you should consider is supportability. When you do pick a specialty, pick one with backbone. Pick one that can be reused again and again—that will keep on inspiring interest over and over. That will fit up-offering with different items and additionally updates. And keeping in mind that you do that, attention on how you offer, not just what you offer, with the goal that you can re-utilize what you realize. That way, you can keep on being a Big Shot affiliate achievement well into the future (say, to retirement?) even as items and affiliate programs travel every which way.

If at this point you are concerned and considering, "Amazing. Presently I simply don't realize what to offer, and I thought I had everything made sense of… " don't stress. This book is here to re-prepare you and instruct you to offer and profit the manner in which the Big Shots do. Not the manner in which the general population influencing streams and spots of affiliate cash to do, the manner in which the general population living off affiliate commissions do. Also, keeping that in mind, we will absolutely clarify for you how to identify the items that will offer. Actually, we'll do that without further ado. But first, how about we take away another dread.

But I'm no master

Affirm, so now that we've expelled the prospect of offering specialty items that you like, and taken away your programmed level of comfort with your item, we have to discuss how to revise that issue for you, yes?

It is significantly simpler to offer something you know and love, unquestionably. It is less demanding—in any event at the outset—to construct marketing and pre-deals around an item you have an enthusiasm for; which means, if you are as of now a specialist in "widgetta obscura" you could likely take a seat and in one evening draft an entire site brimming with substance on the issue. What's more, if you pick another item, say a sought after high dealer that you know alongside nothing about, you'll need to do some examination before you can belt out that substance. You'll need to wind up a specialist once more.

There. You've quite recently been given the appropriate response. Did you see it? Turn into a specialist. Similarly as you were not conceived a specialist in gadgets, similarly as you turned into a specialist through examination and utilize, you can do a similar thing for any item that with phenomenal purchaser request.

Everything necessary to end up a specialist is some time spent perusing, and in the long run utilizing your items. You can turn into a specialist. You can turn into whatever sort of master you need to be. What's more, trust us when we say that you need to be the master who knows the items with prepared to-purchase customers.

That being stated, there is something more to think of you as—don't generally should be a specialist to be a viable affiliate! As a matter of course it is very likely you'll wind up one after some time, but meanwhile you should simply give your parent a chance to affiliate program take every necessary step for you! All the data and requesting and buying instruments are now there for you. Your activity is simply to get your kin to them so they can purchase. Also, trust us when we say that if you focus on the correct markets, they're probably going to accompany a lot of data in any case!

The special cases to the standard

We said there would be special cases to the standard of picking a specialty that interests you. That exemption is extremely straightforward, and we won't invest a great deal of energy in it here.

The exemption to the standard is that if you happen to adore an item that individuals are climbing to purchase, put it all on the line! Bounce in now while the getting is great. View yourself as fortunate.

The other special case is your own advantage. If you feel a passionate longing to advance an item inside your specialty to suit your very own extravagant, go for that, as well! There are no standards to what you can and can't offer. You can be a web advertiser of a large number of immensely different items in a wide range of specialties. Truth be told, that is most likely a smart thought. There is nobody immaculate specialty, there are many. Open up your alternatives, do your fanciful things as an afterthought, but plan to profit the manner in which the Big Shots do—by offering the correct items that require minimal measure of exertion on their part.

The most effective method to spot a moneymaker when you see one

Fine. You can acknowledge that you can't become showbiz royalty pitching your gadgets to the five other individuals who love gadgets. You acknowledge that you need to search for the item that is popular, with purchasers prepared to click that "purchase" button. So how would you know which items to pick?

This is the place your affiliate devices come in. This is the place focused on item inquire about comes in. This is likewise where SEO and catchphrase investigate begins to come into the image, but the subtle elements of every one of those will come in their due time, in their own, devoted parts.

Recognizing the dealers

What you have to do to recognize a moneymaker is discover what is offering and what isn't. Go to affiliate destinations like Click Bank and Commission Junction. Use the commercial center apparatuses there and discover what items are performing—which items different affiliates are profiting with. Begin there, but go further. Consider the entire picture before you settle on the correct affiliate items for you.

Go to these destinations, and take a gander at the market reports. Don't simply begin with a best catchphrase look; discover what is offering—not exactly what is getting activity hits. Look at items in your picked class against one another. See which items are outflanking the others, and after that go from that point. Construct your site and your affiliate program around that item. At that point utilize your catchphrase examination in the most profitable route (as we'll demonstrate you).

Here's the trap, however. You would prefer not to simply get the primary items you see with the most elevated activity ages.

What offers and what doesn't

Once in a while these insights are things that you can discover through the commercial center instruments on affiliate lead locales. Not generally, however, and a few destinations are greater at it than others, so you have to take a gander at the demonstrated elements that will probably result in deals. The secret to this is truly in knowing somewhat about the brain research of purchasers, and afterward utilizing that to control your endeavors at SEO and marketing (but more on that later...).

Leading comprehend that there are essentially just two sorts of purchasers important to you; they are

- Buyers who are investigating items, and

- Buyers who require an item (or feel they require an item) since they require an answer for an issue (or think purchasing tackles an issue—some of the time the issue is straightforward need)

Are there different sorts of movement generators out there? Beyond any doubt. But the vast majority of them are not purchasers who are prepared or about prepared to purchase.

With the goal that sort of activity is basically cushion. meter, but it doesn't profit. also, exertion.

It looks great on your site, so it's not worth your time

This is the place catchphrase inquire about truly becomes possibly the most important factor. Compelling watchword research will focus on those purchasers prepared to purchase, as opposed to those simply glancing around. We'll separate that in later parts.

It might appear just as we've made tracks in an opposite direction from the issue of specialty choice. Truly, however, it's everything interlaced. To pick your specialty—since you're not picking on intrigue alone—you should know how to pick the specialties that can perform. You have to know how to recognize the moneymakers, utilizing your market devices.

Getting Your Site Up, Running, and Making Money

Getting affiliate joins is the simple part. Having a place to have them—now that is somewhat more included. Having a place to have them where individuals will change over to purchasers—that is much more work. You have to make a place where individuals can discover you, where they'll need to want data or help, and where they'll leave just to go finish the deal (despite the fact that they may not understand they are 'clearing out'). By and by, it tends to be finished. But before you do anything, you have to structure a course of action. You have to compose the arrangement that gives all of you the potential for offering that you require.

But first, your arrangement

We won't broadly expound on how and where to get a genuine site—that is data you can discover effortlessly enough and potentially as of now have. We'll toss out two or three names like GoDaddy and HostGator, but additionally realize that there are various hosts and site building layouts extending from the complimentary gift that accompanied your ISP to being your very own host. The main point you have to know is that anybody can manufacture a serviceable, appealing site; and regardless of whether it's not the most attractive on the square, if it's fabricated so movement can come, they will.

What we need to center around more is the structure of your site and additionally sites. For one thing, we'll discuss the individual locales themselves.

If you will advance in excess of one item—and to profit the manner in which the Big Shots do you should—each related gathering of items ought to have their very own committed site; out of that gathering, you will center around your one most encouraging item more often than not. This site doesn't should be tremendous, it very well may be only a couple of pages altogether—say somewhere in the range of ten and twenty, contingent upon the quantity of items you'll be offering; but it needs to consolidate every one of the components that will pick up you consideration from the web indexes, and accordingly from guests and purchasers (directed purchasers with a need!).

In the end you will need to fabricate an ace site that coordinates to every one of your littler, item engaged sites. This will be the site you use to "tidy up" whatever remains of the activity produced by the catchphrases you haven't focused on—those all inclusive statements that aren't really nearly purchasing anything. But that can come later. To begin with, construct the destinations that will offer and begin profiting sooner.

So at first, your arrangement will look something like this:

- Target markets and watchwords

- Choose specific affiliate items

- Build a site around a specific gathering of items

- Build more item gathered sites for every association

- Create an ace site that catches activity, at that point joins movement to littler item specific sites

How about we attempt to place this into point of view and give you a genuine model.

Affirm; how about we guess that you are offering wellness related items—an assortment of sorts from lifting weights enhancements to fifteen moment exercise schedules. The purchasers who are searching for muscle-building enhancements and powders could likely think less about your time to get down to business exercise recordings. Furthermore, you don't look like quite a bit of a solid expert by simply slapping up one promotion beside the other. So you separate every one of those item composes into gatherings, and market five or six or so together on one site devoted to each. So as opposed to having a catch-all site with wellness items, you have two committed sites that specifically serve the necessities of the guests prepared to purchase. You have

- A 10-20 page site offering working out enhancements, and

- A 10-20 page site offering exercise recordings for the as well occupied to-practice swarm

Each site gives your purchasers what they require—not what alternate needs. After those locales are built up and doing their thing, you can return to that model of the wellness items store, and make segments and virtual "walkways" that point to these littler committed destinations.

Presently here we have to clarify a bit. This structure is one of the main things that Big Shot affiliates do, and little players don't.

What you will see ordinarily is that little players gather various items, normally related, now and again not even, and amass them all on one site. They advertise their affiliate site as a kind of one-quit shopping customer facing facade for everything. Furthermore, they make so much perplexity and rivalry among their very own affiliate items that they never expand the capability of the business movement that is coming in.

What the Big Shots do interestingly is begin by concentrating on the little destinations. They develop items in a way that plainly offers every one. They make decision for purchasers by looking at their own like-items against one another, with the goal that whatever item is picked, the deal is theirs. Virtuoso, yes?

At that point they get the movement going to and purchasing at those destinations. Later on they'll fabricate something more similar to the retail facade, and connection to these littler locales when guests snap to take in more, just to tidy up whatever remains of the lookers.

At last, in the long run in any case, both the Big Shots and little clocks both wind up with catch-all parent destinations, but the Big Shots have that additional layer of offers security that gives the clients what they have to make the deal, and furthermore gets movement at the two finishes.

Presently construct it and they'll come

What you most need to know, at that point, is the manner by which to assemble that little specialty site.

To emphasize, the reason for this webpage is to build up an exceptionally buyer specific site that gives data and assets to the individual who is hoping to purchase a result of this compose. That is from the purchaser's point of view. But you have web crawlers to if you don't mind as well, with the goal that substance should do twofold obligation and furthermore enable you to be found and positioned well for your objective watchwords and target gathering of people.

There are two fundamental parts to these little destinations. Those are

1. Articles and purchaser driven data

2. Products

The pages of your site will be part among these two segments. It presumably ought not be a straight 50/50 split. The division ought to be weighted more for data than items. This will fill two needs:

1. Information gives the purchaser all the supporting data and subtle elements they have to choose to purchase.

2. Information gives more feed to web crawlers with the goal that purchasers can discover you.

Anyway you choose to structure the real site, it ought to have a straightforward division—data and items.

The item pages are basic. Make a page for every individual item that gives the specifics on the item (regularly the data given by the affiliate). You have to give enough detail without trying too hard. Set up the item pages with the goal that when the guest plays out the coveted activity—clicks a 'purchase' button, or chooses a free example or administration—they are taken to the affiliate site, where they [hopefully] will request and buy your item.

The instructive pages require somewhat more work, but not all that much. Every one of these pages should have one bit of supporting data which causes your guest choose to purchase. It ought to be an article, item audit, or item correlation. As you'll learn later, these are the things that will truly draw the simple specific and focused on prepared to purchase customers that you need. This is the data that they are searching for only preceding buy, thus the data is destined to net genuine purchasers, and not simply inquisitive guests.

Back to our precedent, if we have five muscle-building supplements, we'll have five pages of items and maybe ten pages with articles and correlations. Utilize the articles to address the worries of individuals in the market for enhancements, and incorporate points critical to them. They may be one next to the other examinations, audits of specific powders, or subjects, for example, "Five Tips for Building More Muscle."

Presently you've given your officially penniless purchasers the two things they have to choose to purchase your items—extra data, and the place to make the buy.

Tips for Tapping into Demand Markets

To be clear, these strategies can and do work to make you offer in any market, paying little respect to how sought after and exceptionally focused the market may appear at first view. The key isn't in going for the most prevalent movement, but in the most focused on activity.

You can, assuredly, increase enough ground in any popularity specialty market to make Big Shot sort of money. For one thing, you're not hoping to net each deal the specialty makes, you're simply hoping to net a rate that converts into enduring wage for you. Sought after business sectors, even a little level of by and large deals can be very productive.

But besides, you—rather than most different affiliates out there—are focusing on the correct sort of movement. You are utilizing the less-frequently looked, but more profitable watchwords to get your movement, thus you've just slipped in under the radar of every other person that has cornered the big deal catchphrases (but are making couple of offers with them).

In web marketing circles, this is what is alluded to as riding the 'long tail' of catchphrases. For each best catchphrase, there are some more (hundreds all the more once in a while) that are utilized via searchers and ignored by site proprietors since they are not the "best" approach to attract huge movement. But the key isn't amount to such an extent as it is quality, so for you that works fine and dandy.

Fundamentally, tapping in to the huge interest showcases all comes down to this:

- Choose specialties that have offering potential—not dark interests where nobody is purchasing (illuminate a need! Give an item)

- Choose the items inside that specialty that are truly offering and that address the issues of your purchasers

- Figure out what the best merchants of those items (your opposition) are doing that serves the necessities of your shoppers; draft a layout of your targeted buyers

- Use the correct catchphrases to pull in the correct sorts of shoppers

- Create content that serves your group of onlookers, and furthermore sustains the web crawlers

Pursue this basic arrangement for tapping the sought after business sectors that are offering and producing affiliate benefits, and afterward you will be extremely well on your approach to profiting effortlessly, much the same as whatever is left of the Big Shot affiliates do.

Chapter 4

Conversion Strategies

All in all, Why Does Conversion Matter?

Individuals regularly need to know—for what reason does transformation make a difference? At the point when at last, transformation is the only thing that is in any way important. If your sites don't change over guests into purchasers, you're simply not profiting. Enough said. Plain and basic. That is the reason change matters.

But to go above and beyond, transformation as it is important to you, the Big Shot affiliate advertiser, isn't just about what a couple of guests do—it's about what the majority at your site do. For our motivations here, change truly implies what your site is doing in general. We can't sensibly anticipate that that each guest will your site will change over into a purchaser (but wouldn't it be decent if we could!). You do need to realize that in general, in any case, what you are doing on your site is working.

Change is about rates and insights and deals, and tragically there are no genuine strong guidelines that apply. You can't make clearing judgments on the grounds that the tenets will be different for every last item that you have. Every item and specialty has its very own arrangement of requirements.

What you can do is expand the benefit of your site. The best approach to do that is to test and change and change your substance and your site until the point when you have gotten the most noteworthy measure of offers and gainfulness that you can. There are approaches to do that, and that is the thing that we'll discuss straightaway, but all things considered there is an unmistakable component of experimentation associated with changing over site guests into purchasers.

At last, we're left with precisely what we began with in reply to this inquiry. Plain and straightforward, transformation matters since change levels with deals. Take in the "craftsmanship" of the transformation, and you'll have one a greater amount of the significant bits of the affiliate marketing riddle.

The most effective method to get it Going

For one thing, to see how to get transformation going, you need to comprehend your job in the fantastic plan of things. Your job—your sole reason for Big Shot survival—is to get your guests to your parent affiliate's business page—your trader's business page.

Numerous new affiliates, and in fact some prepared affiliates who simply don't 'get it', erroneously believe that their activity is to offer the items themselves. Unobtrusively, truly, in manners, that is valid. But by and large, that isn't your activity—the business itself is the job of the item dealer. What you have to do is warm your guests up so they can feel positive about making that last stride, and proceeding to take care of business.

Once more, this is the place you have to understand that the vendor has completed a great deal of the work for you. They've built the business pages and request handling systems. They've composed (or had composed) the executioner duplicate that will absolutely persuade the purchaser to purchase. All they require you to do is get the vender there.

This is the piece of the business that is alluded to as the 'pre deal' or 'pre offering'. This is where you fill in as the center man—the contact between the vender who has this extraordinary item and the purchaser who truly wants to purchase, but needs that additional little push, or the point the correct way.

Something essential to recall, as well, is this—your perusers are occupied individuals. They, similar to you and every other person in the cutting edge world, don't possess the energy for broad perusing and research. That is for what reason they're coming to you. They're seeking you've effectively done that after them. The exercise to take from that will be that you should set up quality, item supporting substance, and you should make it significant; but you ought not slaughter your guests with generosity. Make the entire procedure simple.

- Give perusers a snippet of data they can utilize (an item survey, an instructional exercise, and so on).

- Show them that you comprehend their need (you identify with their concern, you see their need, you know how to settle it, you've been in their shoes).

- Point them to the place with the arrangement (connection to your shipper's page).

- Let the trader wrap up! (They've effectively done it at any rate, why emphasize and squander your guests' time?)

The entire procedure is done and over in around three basic advances. What's more, out of those, the special case that truly requires work is the giving of helpful data—the changing over part. You'll peruse more about some quite certain techniques for unpretentious changes in the last piece of this part in the 'Tips and Tricks' segment, but comprehend that whichever strategy you utilize, it needs to fit inside the necessities and requests of the guest's life. As it were, it should be straightforward, coordinated, and successful. And all the better if it is activity situated. At the point when individuals need to make a move (and we're not simply discussing the activity of purchasing), they believe they are being beneficial and proactive in satisfying their requirements, or taking care of their issues, whichever the case might be for your product(s); here and there it could be both.

Center is Everything

You've manufactured your affiliate site and your pages which is as it should be. An unmistakable reason—to offer your focused on affiliate item! What is basic to your prosperity as an affiliate—to yapping with the Big Shots, not simply slurping up the stream—is to remain centered around that focal objective, that unmistakable driving explanation behind the specific presence of your site.

To do that, you have to watch out for the prize, to utilize another platitude. You need to make your data and your item your main center; all the more specifically, the main core interest.

Very frequently, affiliates are drawn by the possibility of income sans work from easy to utilize adaptation programs like AdSense or some such program. They'll top off their locales with advertisements to profit, and they murder their odds at affiliate achievement!

Essentially what you achieve when you top off your transformation site with promoting and fringe adaptation procedures is welcoming in the entirety of your rivals. Each promotion or connection that posts is one greater open door for your group, which you've endeavored to arrive, to leave and get devoured by the digressions. You drive your own one of a kind guests straight into the pausing, completely open arms of your opposition!

In addition, the consideration of different promotions and floods of data is down right confounding. You attract your guests with the guarantee of the data they've so urgently looked for, and after that you take them to a site so obfuscated with standard promotions and connections that they can't tell which one is the piece they've wanted. They end up diverted and disappointed. And afterward they clear out. They return to their pursuit bar to discover a site that truly conveys the merchandise.

Trust us when we say (and you most likely know this fair from being a web customer yourself) that individuals have had enough of counterfeit destinations that don't encourage them. They need the site that is direct, to the point, and encourages them, as opposed to obstructs them. They perceive the actors inside a couple of moments of arriving on a site, and if you don't turn out to be useful immediately, they'll proceed onward and not try to look down for your article or item audit to see whether it truly is there.

How, at that point, do you make center around your site pages?

- Stay far from promoting, adaptation programs, and outward connections that don't prompt your business pages (at your trader's site)

- Only incorporate promotions and connections that go to your affiliate items (imbedded, normally, with your affiliate ID so the deal is credited to you)

- Feature your limited time material and one connection over the overlap of the page with the goal that it is promptly accessible (seen quickly by guests when they arrive on your page) maintain the emphasis on the arrangement your perusers look for

Keep in mind that this center is about useful substance. This isn't the place for the hard-offer direct mail advertisement. Leave that to your shipper. This is the place for delicate offering; the sort of offering a companion of yours strength do by proposing something that is worked for him or her.
Remain concentrated on your objective and concentrated on the item and arrangement within reach. Thusly, you'll enable your guests to look after center, and move them on to where your genuine benefits lie.

Tips and Tricks You Can Use

You have the hypothesis down, so at this point no uncertainty you're searching for some genuine systems that you can use to enable you to change over web activity into purchasing, paying clients at your shipper's website. Here are a portion of the things that the Big Shots do that you can do too to profit… in the affiliate's way!

Make Interactive Experiences

As we stated, individuals feel a feeling of achievement from activity. What's more, it doesn't should be intricate activity, either. Indeed, even a basic activity, such as utilizing a survey or symptomatic test, can give that sentiment of achievement that gets guests one bit nearer to purchasing.

If you truly consider it, the whole procedure is simply many actions—one stage prompting another; first,

- Visitor has a need or an issue, for which they require an answer

- Visitor begins looking for answers for his/her concern, or items to satisfy his/her need

- Visitor taps on your site in a pursuit, since it apparently offers something accommodating of significant worth

- Visitor peruses your substance, at that point...

... What comes next is dependent upon you. If you figure out how to make it another activity step, your guest will keep on liking what he or she is doing. So perhaps you set up a little test or poll that presents the issues they are confronting. You reveal to them that if they take this a couple of inquiry test, you can enable them to take care of their concern. Possibly you offer a preliminary rendition to demonstrate how you can help (which prompts a preliminary at your trader's site), or perhaps you entice them by motivating them to make a move now with the goal that they can appreciate a special reward—a free program or item that you've made, just to include esteem and get the deal.

These activities can enable you to change over purchasers by unpretentiously moving them on to your vendor's business page. Also, the best part is, your guests will be glad you're doing it, since you are helping them!

Alongside this, you can utilize other little tips and little-known techniques that have been known to increment clicking, and subsequently increment transformations. A few precedents…

- Divide articles and instructional exercises crosswise over pages so guests need to go starting with one then onto the next, (for example, by clicking a 'Next' button, and so forth)

- Place arrange buttons or connections as elective choices alongside other activity buttons, (for example, with the 'following' button)

- Use different activity buttons put deliberately on your pages; they have a tendency to show signs of improvement reaction than connections and make the guest feel they are proceeding onward to better things (despite the fact that they'll all prompt a similar place)

- Use extra highlights like special codes to enable guests to feel they are getting an additional

- Give an additional reward, for example, an adding machine or converter you've fabricated or had constructed, something that associates with your item (for instance, for wellness items, maybe a calorie converter or burner)

- Assign an activity off-site, for example, utilizing the free capacity at site ABC (your shipper's site)

- Lay out a bigger arrangement of activity, and spell out the means your guests should take to fathom his/her concern

- Use instructional exercises with different activity ventures, sooner or later including your item

- Use recordings to exhibit item employments

Most importantly, regardless of what procedure you choose to utilize, keep your site's route clear and straightforward. Make it evident what your peruser needs to do, and make it simple for him to do it. Utilize clear, easy to use transformation activities to advance individuals and land them on that purchase button on your vendor's page.

A Closer Look at the Blogosphere

What is the blogosphere, truly? It's where anybody—man, lady, youngster, or mechanized feed scrubber—can slap up formats or fabricate their very own site and refresh it with helpful(?) data or stories of their week by week shopping outings to their souls content. It's both an intense device used by organizations and sites on a day by day (or all the more frequently) premise and a running individual journal set up online for all to see. The blogosphere is loaded up with specialists and learners, and individuals who think they are specialists who are truly fledglings. It's a blended sack of substance and ability, or deficiency in that department. It's a network encounter that knows no genuine limits. Or on the other hand limits.

Thusly, web journals can be a help or a bust to your affiliate program. By and by, they are being touted as the quickest, least demanding, most oversimplified approach to advance affiliate items and produce deals.

But would they say they are? How about we investigate the two sides of this issue.

The up-side. How about we investigate what we have; blogging is

- Easy to begin

- Cheap to begin

- An simple place to set up important data that can truly have an incentive for your perusers

- A put where you can use the network perspectives, for example, remarking to hold virtual discussions with your perusers

- A put where you can conceivably fabricate long haul associations with your perusers, which thus can help return deals and add to the lifetime estimation of that client

- A put where you can include, in detail and inside and out, any particular item you need

- A basic approach to refresh substance to get on the great side of web crawlers

That is a significant rundown of benefits in the contention for blogging. Honestly, blogging is—or can be, can possibly be—these things and most likely more. A blog can be a decent method to offer an affiliate item. But there are a considerable measure of different things that online journals are, as well, and huge numbers of these characteristics don't fit into the more fantastic plan of affiliate sites. So before we settle on whether to blog or not to blog, we should takes a gander at the other side of the coin.

Why Blogging Might be a Bust

A significant number of the specific things that make blogging a 'characteristic' decision for affiliate advancements are what make blogging the wrong method to adequately advertise as an affiliate.

As a matter of first importance, we should go up against the very blogosphere itself. It's a swarmed place. The facts confirm that the blogosphere is loaded up with an assortment of interests, and holds something for everybody, but amidst such intrigue, it's inexorably difficult to be found. Indeed, even the best, most prolific, and most committed bloggers take months and years to fabricate a strong after. A blog is in no way, shape or form the place to go for moment activity.

The people group part of blogging can be extraordinary, but wouldn't it be able to likewise be a failure? All that remarking and free-for-all outside analysis may neutralize you and ruin you. What's more, you have to think about how significant that following is. This will to a great extent rely upon your range of item contributions. If you have an assortment of items that a client should need to return for, or an upgradeable item suite, keeping in contact with purchasers could be an extraordinary thing. If your item is to a greater extent a one-time-just buy, there's likely no recovering the time speculation you will bring about.

Content refreshment is one of the greatest perceived benefits of blogging. You can post rapidly and effortlessly regular and in this way satisfy those web crawlers and hungry blog-adherents with new substance. There's no denying that. But you have to thoroughly consider this—what amount would you be able to concoct to say in regards to your items? Would you be able to keep your items forthright on a blog? How frequently would you be able to turn it? What's more, in particular, what happens when your well of points becomes scarce? Those web indexes and perusers will sit tight for additional, and you'll be getting a handle on for new post thoughts.

It's anything but difficult to kick a blog off and keep it running for a couple of months, but Big Shot sort of wage requests that you develop an all the more long haul plan. Hypothetically a blog is a long haul prospect, but without something new to state, one can just live so long.

We additionally need to handle the issue of having the capacity to highlight different items. This flies right even with the dialog we simply had in the last part, isn't that right? By doing that, you're separating your powers and removing the concentration from your best seeded endeavors.

You've made a commercial center of perplexity, and you've made it difficult to make sense of what the right—basic—arrangement is.

We likewise need to discuss web journals from an auxiliary outlook. Except if you can assemble your own blog (and regardless of whether you can this is intense…), web journals and layouts don't take into account an abnormal state of adaptability. There is an essential structure, and it is difficult to include the buttons and highlights in the spots you require them to be. Consider that occasionally the structure and configuration you've buckled down for might be affected (modified) by the length and measure of your postings.

Presently it may seem like we're totally hostile to blogging for affiliate programs, but that is not actually the situation. How about we wrap this dialog up by taking a gander at how a blog may in any case be a helpful instrument.

Websites are not horrendous things. They are not the most despicable aspect of the affiliate. But there is excessively about a blog that makes it unmanageable as a sole offering specialist for affiliate items.

To be clear, we are not by any means against blogging. There is a place for the individuals who appreciate it, and a helpfulness that can absolutely support affiliate deals. But that place is auxiliary to the structure we've effectively laid out here. Similar to the deals that you will produce however a blog.

The separation that you get from a blog, even given their numerous benefits, does not merit the speculation of time and exertion; not from the angle of your essential offering device. Or maybe, you would be in an ideal situation consigning a blog to an auxiliary feeder-wellspring of activity and income.

It takes a great deal of steady, devoted work to be a blogger and to keep up a blog reliably in the manner in which that will net these benefits for you. Blogging is a considerable measure of diligent work—and it never closes, or your salary stream will. What's more, plain and basically, that is simply not what being a Big Shot affiliate is about. Being a Big Shot isn't tied in with buckling down for your cash, it's tied in with buckling down for fourteen days, and afterward riding the coattails of your prosperity. It's about least support. Also, a blog isn't that. Blogging is an approach to profit as an affiliate, but it's not the Big Shot way.

In summation, if you appreciate blogging let it all out! But don't make it the focal point of your affiliate strategy for success.

Different Options that can Pay Off More

Ideally we haven't dashed your fantasies too hopeless in the area of being a major accomplishment by blogging your approach to enormous affiliate deals. But you came here to figure out how to be a Big Shot Super Affiliate, not to discover how to make streaming deals; so we need to offer it to you straight.

Perceiving that we may have quite recently put a major scratch in your approach, let us make up for ourselves by offering you some wise counsel. We should discuss how your blogging endeavors may be better spent for greater deals and profits for your time venture.

Site and Content

The conspicuous decision is put that exertion into your site and substance. You can accomplish similar outcomes by essentially invigorating the substance of your site. You can add to its chronicles and extra assets segments (without muddying the essential pages we built up previously), and still give ebb and flow data and extra incentive to your clients and to the web indexes.

Not exclusively would you be able to include extra substance, but you can test and change and change the substance you have and test it against past forms. As you'll learn, even little, apparently insignificant changes can truly have a major effect to movement and transformations. Invest the energy you would spend presenting on a blog on search for ways that you can change or improve your site.

Also, bear in mind—you have that ace site to construct. Rather than giving time to a negligible return blog, why not begin on your huge catch-all with the goal that you can overwhelm your specialty movement?

Articles, Articles and More Articles

Every one of the articles you compose, or procure out to an independent author to have composed, don't should be posted on your site. Truth be told, they shouldn't be. Utilize those essential articles and instructional exercises on your site, include some new stuff once in a while to keep everybody glad, and afterward submit to article registries. Use profile and connection abilities to interface back to your site, the expert on Widgets. (You may know this technique by other famous names, similar to "Bum Marketing" or "Article Marketing.")

Endorser Lists and Mailings

This is something you have to take some mind with. Endorser records are not suggested for a wide range of items; leastwise, building your rundown through crush pages isn't prescribed for everybody. For some locales, the nearness of a press page between the site and shipper offer will just turn the guest of, and ask them to take a hike to the following, less requesting supplier.

All things considered, there are approaches to make endorser records work. If your item fits this sort of offers, at that point invest energy making incredible messages and marketing efforts.

Social Marketing

Social marketing is what is driving web 2.0. Rather than investing your energy in another blog individuals could conceivably in the end find, spend it on the web journals of others who've just caught your crowd. Turn into a contributing individual from the network, make a few companions, and utilize your mind and insight to inspire individuals to tap on your name, connection, or profile and visit your site. Do likewise by making pages on social sites like Squidoo and MySpace; visit gatherings and different spots where potential purchasers may assemble.

By taking part in social marketing, you're conveying your items to the majority, as opposed to sitting tight for them to discover you. It's a significantly more dynamic methodology, and one that can be custom fitted to offer that immensely vital center your affiliate plan needs. That, as well as it's significantly more fun than conversing with yourself on your blog, as well, and you won't need to stress over keeping up it when you're off in the midst of some recreation getting a charge out of all that Big Shot affiliate money!

Since we've tended to the topic of blogging, we should proceed onward and discuss the one thing that overwhelms the web—playing the web diversion to pull in the rush hour gridlock. In the following couple of parts, we'll discuss how to keep running with the Big Shots that run the entire show—Google and its associates (if Google has a genuine companion... .). Next, we'll get into the issue of web search tools and improving to make them your companions. It's significant to affiliate marketing, so don't miss these next couple of scenes.

Chapter 5

Google and Fast Traffic Secrets

Why Search Engine Traffic Matters to You

We can't be clearer. Without web crawler activity, you have no movement by any means; none worth making reference to and absolutely insufficient to manage your affiliate business.

At least 90% of the movement to your website(s) will be from web indexes, fundamentally the enormous names like Google, Yahoo!, and MSN. These web crawlers are what will convey hundreds or thousands of individuals to your virtual doorstep looking for items and data, for example, that you've given.

Outside of web indexes, sites create movement in just a couple of ways. These incorporate

- Links from different sites or articles

- Links and addresses from customary marketing

- The periodic informal introduction

These consolidated, notwithstanding, just liken to around 10% of guest movement. And keeping in mind that 10% is positively something worth snatching, the most perfect use of your assets is upgrading for web crawler activity. (By chance, your endeavors to improve will put more connections and presentation out there for your site to be found through the previously mentioned means, making internet searcher focused advancement significantly more essential.)

All the more critically, the activity that you get from a web index is natural. That just implies that the activity that web indexes produce for you is movement from genuine, live individuals out hunting down a webpage like yours. They scan for data and items to serve a need. That need might get, it might learn, business advancement, critical thinking or what have you, but everything boils down to a certain something—these are the general population that are running on the web with the express reason for discovering somebody like you.

While the individuals who tap on connections or enter your web address from a business card or some such means may simply be interest searchers, the general population originating from web indexes began with a reason, an objective as a primary concern. What's more, if you're great, regardless of whether that essential objective wasn't getting, you could conceivably persuade them that that is truly what they were after from the beginning, and you very well might get that deal!

Some web indexes matter more than others

We've built up that the main way somebody looking through the tremendous hills of data on the web can discover you [without a location or connection access] is by utilizing an internet searcher. 90% of guests, maybe more, will discover you along these lines. But as the vast majority of us additionally know, there are many, many web indexes out there, and not every one of them are the equivalent. A bunch of web crawlers matter a ton more than the rest.

So who matters and who doesn't? In truth, everybody matters in light of the fact that each appearance created by even the most dark web search tool matters. But for your motivations, you have to work to satisfy the Big Shots in the hunt world with the goal that you get the a lot of the scans for your focused on watchwords and key expressions.

Having said that, comprehend that there is just so much you can do. Pursue the exhortation given in ensuing sections here so you rank well in the more prominent web crawler results pages (SERP's), and the rest will practically pursue in any case.

Web search tools that standard the web

Enough talking around it, how about we investigate who truly matters in the web crawler world.

As per seoconsultants.com, the main ten US web crawlers are:

1. Google

2. Yahoo!

3. MSN

4. AOL Search

5. Ask

(Second level web indexes recorded one after another in order, not arranged by execution)

- Alta Vista

- Fast

- Gigablast

- Netscape Search

- Snap.com

What's more, as per information gathered by seoconsultants.com from a Hitwise official statement, the breakdown of activity share by significant web indexes resembles this:

- Google—67%

- Yahoo!— 20%

- MSN—7%

- Ask—4%

Include these numbers up, and you'll see that around 98% of quests are created by only four noteworthy web indexes. That, as well as of the second-level entertainers, and even some in the initial, a few littler motors are fueled by the significant motors. For instance, AOL Search is controlled by Google, as is Netscape; Alta Vista and Netscape are fueled by Yahoo!

The exercise to learn, at that point, is to work to satisfy the real players, and the rest should fall in line. Also, regardless of whether they don't, you'll get to the best level of web searchers, and that is your definitive objective.

How everything Works, or Doesn't

Normally, to see how to satisfy these web indexes and rank well in the SERP's, or Search Engine Rank Pages, you need an essential comprehension of how everything functions (or, if you treat it terribly, how it doesn't!). Until further notice, we'll give you that fundamental comprehension. Later on in the part on SEO (section 8), we'll speak specifically about the sort of watchword choice that will work to get you found and get you activity.

Driving web indexes

What drives web search tools are their very own ordering programs. Those ordering programs are encouraged data from projects which slither the a huge number of pages on the web and input fundamental data to the motor. These crawlers are most usually alluded to as 'Insects'. The correct projects and calculations utilized by these projects are not uncovered, and differ from internet searcher to web crawler. But from training and study, we can decide the most essential, and even a portion of the more mind boggling, hones utilized by the significant web indexes.

At the point when arachnids go creeping the web, they begin with the most famous pages. From that point, they pursue the structure and connections from those destinations to different pages and sites, ordering the frequently happening words as they come.

What the bugs consider to be the more essential watchwords—and for some random subject there can be many—they send back to their database. There, those watchwords and expressions are classified, and data is kept to rapidly advise the web search tool where to discover the words and going with data once more, for example, when a client enters those terms or comparative terms into a pursuit bar.

In light of an assortment of variables, the pages that host the data, or words, that the arachnids find are positioned in significance and importance to a subject, or all the more precisely, an arrangement of terms; if in excess of one arrangement of terms shows up on a site, the site can be positioned for those terms, giving the likelihood to rank well for some related, but different arrangements of catchphrases or key expressions.

What's recorded and what isn't

Talking basically of the real web search tools, what are ordered are the more significant words on the webpage. Relational words and 'filler' words, for example, an, a, the, in, and so on, are disregarded. What the bugs search for are the words that show up on the site that really mean something to the end client.

Those words can show up for all intents and purposes anyplace on the site. The insects will look content, features, sidebars, promotions, and coded labels in the background. A portion of these words will include more weight if utilized legitimately. For instance, titles and captions add weight to catchphrases, so it is a smart thought to utilize your essential key expressions in titles and captions and in the Meta labels for the site.

There is something of a craftsmanship to this, be that as it may. It didn't take ache for the web crawlers to make sense of that individuals were essentially stuffing pages with catchphrases and key expressions to get positions and hits, thus they created calculations (undisclosed) to manage the arachnids and reveal to them what is genuine substance and what is counterfeit.

What's more, there are a few kinds of substance that creepy crawlies can't or won't file. They won't record data that you instruct them to overlook (through your coding); content that isn't open since it is limited behind a secret key or security framework can't be gotten to thus won't be crept and positioned. This is a piece of the reason that press pages have restricted convenience, at any rate as far as web index rankings; if the arachnid can't go past that divider, it can't perceive what is behind it. Accordingly, you must have the heft of your advanced substance forthright where the creepy crawly can get at it. Likewise, creepy crawlies have quit positioning a considerable measure of crush pages since they don't offer genuine esteem—they're simply enrollment docs, thus you ought not depend too vigorously on these from a SEO outlook except if you intend to include some substance that will satisfy the bug (and still be helpful to the human shopper, as well).

Modules, non-HTML designs, and non-content substance can't be recorded via web indexes. This implies if you are including any of the accompanying, it may not be filed.

- Plug-in projects

- Videos

- Audios

- Flash documents

- Images

- Photos

- Frames

- Java applets

Obviously, these components can be imperative to the people who utilize your site, and positively do have a reason that warrants utilizing them, but from a SEO outlook, they have next to zero esteem. In this way, the best guidance for affiliates is to keep it basic, form it solid, and limit the utilization of highlights that have restricted return.

To total everything up, everything comes down to this:

- Search results depend on substance and catchphrases.

- Content = Food for web search tools/creepy crawlies

- Quality Content = Good Search Rankings

Since no human would have a petition of finishing such a stupendous undertaking as assessing and ordering every one of the destinations on the web, we need to depend on the best procedures and projects the web indexes can make. Those best projects depend on what adds up to an expand coordinating diversion that matches seek words to words on a page. Basically, if you have no words, or if nothing else no words that issue to arachnids and the general population seeking, you don't have anything to coordinate to, thus you have no chance to get for an internet searcher to discover you.

To rank well in the real web search tools, you have to focus on a select gathering of watchwords and key expressions that you need to rank for. You have to utilize those effectively to demonstrate to the web indexes that you are one of the experts in your subject, for your picked expressions. As made reference to, we'll give you those subtle elements in Chapter 8 when we speak more about SEO. For the present, comprehend the essential inward workings of the web, and begin pondering how you can make that function for you.

Freeware, Shareware, and Other Tricks that Pay

Viral marketing is one of the most effortless and most ideal approaches to produce a lot of inbounds joins (which those web crawlers love) and movement to your site. What's more, the best thing about it is, you can utilize viral marketing techniques to increase quick, simple movement for a little speculation—even free! If you figure out how to saddle this straightforward strategy for using freeware, shareware, and other viral subtle strategies, you'll have adapted one more of the Big Shot approaches to profit from the solace of your shoreline seat.

What is Viral Marketing?

Infections are not regularly invited in either processing or human circles. An infection is a contamination—a malady—a thing to be stayed away from no matter what. In fact, infections are to be entirely stayed away from. But we can gain from the propensities for infections, and make their courses our own to tackle propelled web activity.

At its most fundamental, viral marketing is just the spreading of data starting with one individual then onto the next. It depends on the idea that all things considered, a man will enlighten three others concerning an item that they like. So for each customer you it would be ideal if you there are three more possibilities following behind.

In web circles, this has been connected in a more extensive sense to incorporate informal battling as well as genuine projects that get go around and delighted in; and when those small projects connect to another, more valuable site or item, the viral impact proceeds to in the long run net the ultimate objective, which for this situation is movement to your site, and change of activity into offers of included affiliate items.

Utilizing Freeware and Shareware in Viral Marketing

Battles

Individuals love getting something to no end. That is the reason freeware and shareware are so prominent on the web today. There are whole sites committed to simply giving without end freeware and shareware, and they are making oodles of cash by doing it—as are the general population who claim those projects.

By giving endlessly a free form of a complimentary program that fits in with your affiliate item, you can produce a lot of viral activity into your site. What's incredible about this sort of activity is that it is free of web looks. At the end of the day, the viral movement from freeware is notwithstanding natural activity created via web indexes.

The fundamental technique that is utilized here is this:

- First, you make or have made a straightforward programming application that will engage your objective purchaser. This should be something that ties in with your affiliate item somehow, and that can upgrade the item or help answer addresses which lead the purchaser to your item page.

o For instance, running again with the wellness subject we began before, if you are offering weight training supplements you may make a freeware item that enables your clients to track their exercises and advancement.

•   Next, you make a site for your freeware item. This page will list the item includes and will give download guidelines to the guest with the goal that he or she can truly get the freeware item advertised. But it additionally interfaces somehow to your affiliate item. There are an assortment of ways you can interface out to your shipper's page. Your philosophy will depend a great deal on your affiliate item, and furthermore on the freeware item that you are putting forth.

o For the situation of the exercise tracker, you may just promote your affiliate item site, or offer connects to educational assets. For instance, you may conspicuously show include articles which detail helpful data for weight lifters. Normally, the articles that are connected will be those facilitated on your principle item affiliate site, or, in other words up to change over your guest over to your vendor's page.

o If you have made something like a test or poll style indicative device, the "arrangement" will interface specifically back to either your affiliate site, or all the more presumably your dealer's site—the genuine response to the issue! So for instance here you may make a conclusion apparatus for weight lifters intended to reply "For what reason wouldn't i be able to make gains?" You get some information about exercise propensities, demonstrate that you comprehend the inconvenience confronting the client—for example, no increases regardless of standard, arranged exercises, and after that recommend that a dietary need may be at fault, or that supplementation may help. To take in more about what your body needs, click straightaway.

- Now that you've made your application, you have to put it in frameworks where clients can discover it. Simply, you will submit it to free download locales, for example, freedownloadscenter.com, Tucows.com, or any of around 600+ other free download sites. The sites will offer a concise depiction and outline of the item (which you will make before accommodation) and after that offer a connection to the landing page where the free download exists. That landing page is where your business start!

You can utilize Shareware applications similarly, just as opposed to advancing an affiliate program you are advancing a program that you possess or have made. It begins as a free form, but works for a constrained measure of time before it times out, or has restricted usefulness. The objective is to get your clients to begin to look all starry eyed at your little program with the goal that they do purchase the extra highlights or buy the program after the preliminary time (you'll perceive this as the MO of many driving programming organizations—motivate them to depend on your item so they need to purchase the full form).

Helpful traps and tips for distributing Freeware and Shareware Easily

To attempt to present your applications to all the significant free download focuses would be completely unmanageable. You could sensibly deal with a couple physically and all alone, but that would not be sufficient to truly gain by the activity potential made by making your own freeware and shareware projects and applications. The best way to truly do this is to utilize an accommodation program or something to that affect.

There are different choices out there, for example, FastSubmit, PromoSoft, SharewareTracker and some more. These sorts of items enable you to submit to somewhere in the range of 400 and 600 download locales consequently or semi-naturally, contingent upon the program you pick. You can look into these projects, or just scan for mass-accommodation programming to discover a program that functions admirably for you. A considerable lot of these depend on your having made a PAD record with the required data the download locales will utilize, so you ought to take in more about PAD records and making them if you intend to utilize mass-accommodation programming.

Since you currently know the nuts and bolts of how to use the viral abilities of freeware and shareware, we should talk slightly about producing the thoughts that will make this value your while, and about how you can begin regardless of whether you are totally tech-oblivious.

Creating Winning Ideas

The one thing that you need to remember is that your application needs to somehow engage your group of onlookers. It must be something they will be cheerful to have for nothing. At the end of the day, while they won't expect premium programming in vain (the conceivable special case being shareware programs), they will expect a pleasant small something to no end—the main reason they'll be looking in any case!

There is another thing to remember, as well. It needs to fit with your item/specialty! You can't simply toss out a free credit number cruncher to offer your lifting weights supplements; you must have something that a muscle head will be occupied with having. Something that takes care of an issue, upgrades your item, or helps make his/her working out life simpler.

To enable you to produce new thoughts if you haven't any of your own, approval and hunt around the net and the download destinations. See what other individuals are putting forth in your specialty—particularly those sorts of items that are getting downloaded regularly (you can perceive how frequently a program is downloaded when you tap on it at most destinations) or that have high client audits (once more, accessible on most download locales). Obviously, you can't just take what another person has officially assembled, but you can get a few thoughts and structure one of your own.

Something else, a basic meeting to generate new ideas could create some extraordinary thoughts. Place yourself in your clients' shoes indeed, and consider the things that you may like, or that may make your life simpler.

Simply comprehend that whatever it is you make, it should be something that the two stands without anyone else as a real intuitive item, and one that connections in by one way or another with whatever remains of what you are doing.

Why it works

Understanding why freeware and shareware give-aways work will help you as you produce thoughts and build your applications. What's most vital to comprehend is this—complimentary gifts work since they are intelligent and are of incentive to the client. It's different than making a promotion! It must be something genuine and valuable!

This means you can't simply approach planning an application so far another tedious notice. Applications that are in reality advertisements will just hurt your activity; first in light of the fact that your client will feel tricked, and besides on the grounds that they will be prohibited by the better download locales, and conceivably even outcome in your site being restricted. Hence, the brilliant principle in making freeware applications is to make them something genuine and helpful, fit for remaining without anyone else.

A couple of fundamental tips for making freeware that will net the coveted outcomes are:

- KISS—Keep It Simple, Stupid! Try not to go over the edge; make a basic application without expanding your assets too far. That way if it doesn't get a considerable measure of consideration, you haven't lost much, and that way you additionally don't over-convolute the helpfulness for your clients.

- Quality—make it something that is well-assembled and utilitarian, notwithstanding for its effortlessness.

Substandard items will either not be utilized or will be overlooked by sites.

• Value—incorporate some component of significant worth for your client, whatever it may be, with the goal that you give them a genuine impetus to download your application and utilize it to get to you!

Kicking it into high gear

We told you before in the documentation that it is conceivable to utilize this procedure with practically zero programming learning. To appear you how that is conceivable, we'll discuss only a few choices for making programming efficiently (or for nothing—shockingly better!) and effortlessly.

The most essential freeware applications we are discussing here are very little more than records that connect to the proper target. We're discussing those test style demonstrative surveys that continue for a couple of edges by clicking 'next', and afterward end at the answer for the issue—you dealer site. Else, we could be discussing a connections discoverer or posting operator. You can develop these effectively enough with simply some experimental writing in a HTML editorial manager, some CGI content, and connecting by means of a concealed divert capacity to your preferred URL. You can without much of a stretch learn enough rudiments to do this on the web.

Obviously, more intricate applications may require somewhat more ability and programming aptitude, but if you know where to find that for nothing, you can in any case develop a quality item without a degree in programming. Sites like Freebyte.com, NeedScripts.com, and HotScripts.com all offer free programming contents and codes that can be effectively connected to HTML editors to make uses of a wide assortment of sorts. These free source-codes all by themselves can be an incredible method to create freeware application thoughts.

As should be obvious, with the bounty of projects, free codes and contents, and basic applications that you can expand without anyone else, there are a large number of potential outcomes for even the most mechanically weakened affiliate. So indeed, even you at home can without much of a stretch get this show on the road toward Big Shot benefits!

Chapter 6

SEO and Other Powerful Income Boosting Tools

The Ins and Outs of SEO

Remember we discussed this?

- Search results depend on substance and watchwords.

- Content = Food for web crawlers/bugs

- Quality Content = Good Search Rankings

Well the Ins and Outs of SEO are very little more mind boggling than that. To that, the main thing we may include is the significance of connections:

- Search results depend on substance, catchphrases, and connections

- Links in addition to Content = Food for web indexes/creepy crawlies

- Links in addition to Quality Content = Good Search Rankings

So to outline this part before we even go ahead, if you have great substance that your client is scanning for, and you recover some great connects to your substance, you will rank well in the web crawlers, and you will take advantage of that natural movement which will result in 90% of the activity to your site.

As we said when we talked in regards to how web indexes function, the whole business is governed by coordinating terms to terms—terms on your page to terms guests are searching for. These, and you presumably definitely know this, are what we allude to as watchwords and key expressions. Presently, as you can envision, not every one of the words on your page will extremely matter in light of the fact that nobody is out there scanning for good for nothing words that are all over. What you have to do is make sense of which of the words individuals are hunting down in regard to your specialty and focus on a select gathering of them. These will be the words that you endeavor to advance for, the words that ideally will pick up you SERP positioning close enough to the best to get movement.

These words and expressions will be positioned as a matter of first importance by the substance on your page. That is what is given the most weight and significance via web indexes and by individuals. Furthermore, since site fame, activity, and connecting all says something, as well, content is the most imperative factor in SEO.

Beside SEO endeavors, there is another, more essential motivation to compose content that is helpful and applicable. Your clients! Think about this—nobody cares if you rank first but have nothing to offer after the snap. All that the people care about is regardless of whether you are serving their requirements. After they discover you, if your substance is great they'll remain and examine, utilize your site for some time. If it's simply a heap of catchphrases stacked one upon another, they'll simply leave for the number two-positioned site that really has genuine substance.

Consequently, if you don't comprehend anything else from this section comprehend this—the focal point of all your SEO endeavors should initially be—above whatever else—the nature of your substance! If you don't do anything more than set up great, [humanly] absorbable substance, you've officially accomplished the greater part of what it takes to build up a site that will produce activity.

All things considered, there are different components that say something regarding your positioning that can be enhanced to expand your ubiquity with the web indexes. These incorporate both on location and off-site factors.

On location SEO Components

Three essential parts will choose the main part of your web index rankings. They are

- Content

- Tags

- Link structure

We've practically secured the substance factor. You require quality substance that incorporates those catchphrases at a sensible thickness to satisfy the bugs (to some degree tricky, but somewhere in the range of two and four percent watchword thickness for each term is for the most part acknowledged as the standard and a decent focus on); that substance should satisfy your people all the more essentially, so compose for them and where it bodes well to include your focused on watchwords, do as such, but if it degrades your substance and makes it garbled, let it go.

Labels are the other critical part, as they fill in as somewhat of a guide-framework to web search tool creepy crawlies; that, as well as when you incorporate eye-getting key expressions, your guest's advantage will be aroused also. Be that as it may, quite a bit of what exists in labels is never observed by individuals, so there is more elbowroom here.

Labels are joined to a wide range of substance to disclose it to the arachnids. There are labels for pictures, titles, watchwords, and that's just the beginning. Title labels are the most significant of these, as they have an immediate bearing on your rankings. Title labels fill in as a depiction of the substance on the page. Likewise, the data in the tag shows up in the list items, giving that initially data that the searcher will use to choose which site they need to tap on. Along these lines, title labels are something you need to think about and use as a major aspect of your general SEO crusade.

Meta labels are two or three sentences that portray the substance. Meta labels help put your substance among alternate locales, kind of disclosing it to the internet searcher; they likewise show up in a few ventures to portray the website to the guest. They may bear on SEO, despite the fact that the contention is that their effect is irrelevant. It merits the couple of moments to utilize them, and maybe enter your key terms there, but you ought to be most worried about different parts of SEO.

The third factor in on location SEO is your interior connection structure. From the viewpoint of web crawlers, the better sites have different pages of advantageous substance, and they make safe inner connection structures with the goal that their guests can get around effectively and discover the data they require. That is the thing that you have to work for both your guests and your creepy crawlies.

The inner connection structure ought to be coherent and usable. People will utilize it to peruse all that is important to them, and creepy crawlies will tail them to see where you can take them. Give some thought to this as you fabricate your site, and consider how you can utilize your structure to help all included, and furthermore to coordinate guests and web crawlers where you need them to go.

Notwithstanding simply having the fundamental static segments set up, you additionally need to take care of the elements that influence your page positioning. In every practical sense, those elements are new substance creation. Web search tools like destinations that are state-of-the-art and all around thought about. What's more, from their perspective, locales that are exceptional and very much kept up are destinations that change with the occasions. Hence indeed, refreshing substance is critical.

This does not mean, in any case, that you ought to approach changing your essential substance consistently—only that all the time (and some say day by day is ideal, but what a ton of work that would be! Also, Big Shots aren't into making more work for themselves!) you have to include some new substance. The most effortless approach to do that is hurl another article for the creepy crawlies to bite on. A blog joined to your site can be extremely helpful for this reason. Directed guests looking for help, in any case, will frequently incline toward the convention of an article.

Off-Site SEO Components

That covers the important on location SEO parts; now we have to investigate those off-site factors that bear on your internet searcher prominence.

Web indexes like well known sites. They let the utilization of others demonstrate to them which locales are most worth going to. This shouldn't imply that that you won't be filed by insects before you have in-bound connections built up, it is simply to state that you will rank better when web crawler crawlers can see that others are pointing towards your website, as well.

You can consider it along these lines. The substance on your site gives the nourishment to web indexes—this we've said previously. Furthermore, the connections from others outside your site help web crawlers qualify that, or dole out an incentive to your webpage.

The good to the story is that great connections mean great rankings. You require outside connections coming into your site to increase great positioning and inquiry created activity.

But what makes a decent connection?

The manner in which the crawlers see it, connections ought to pursue a characteristic request. That request goes something like this:

- A site is made

- The site is found by a couple of chance guests

- Those guests like your site, and prescribe it to other people (by connecting, for example, this is the method for spreading uplifting news on the www)

- Those invested individuals tell other invested individuals, and soon there is a safe way of connections starting with one glad client then onto the next, back to your site

Presently its thing is that insects are savvy. They know a characteristic connection structure does not occur in a split second, and it isn't altogether based on one point. So while you can get this show on the road by disseminating a few connections around the web yourself, or exchanging a connection with another person (complementary connections), you can't simply surge a couple of areas with huge amounts of connections back to your site.

Consequently, there are some disqualifiers for the connections coming into your site.

- Off-point joins don't bode well. Cutoff joins from spots that don't share your interests.

- Reciprocal interfaces simply resemble an exchange off, so the majority of your connections can't be picked up in exchange (some weight will be given to shared connections, so they shouldn't be marked down, but don't put every one of your eggs in this crate).

- Having every one of your connections from a couple of sources looks simply like what it is—you out there connecting back to yourself, and not moving around the web to do it. Begin a few connections through social locales like

Squidoo and MySpace, but additionally utilize these for their planned reasons for advising others about your site.

•	Paying for connections from the best sites (since truly, you can pay well known individuals to "like" you) looks similarly devised. Your connection example ought to be from the athletes' table and also the geeks'. Paying for two or three high-hit joins is a decent fire starter, but don't amass your eggs in simply this bin, either.

Fundamentally, you simply need to use interface openings from every classification (connect type—one way, proportional...). A methodology to utilize to build up connections from the outside in might resemble:

•	Establish one-path joins from quality locales

•	Establish proportional connections

•	Submit your site to catalogs

•	Use free article entries (pleasantly suited since they'll disperse over the web and attract joins from everywhere)

•	Engage in interpersonal interaction on point specific specialty discussions and sites, and so on

- Create informal communication pages and focal points at Squidoo, Zimbio, and other comparable locales

This may appear to be practically outlandish, but there are such things as paid connections and connection systems. One that has functioned admirably for some, affiliates is Jonathon Leger's 3WayLinksNetwork. There are others, as well, and you can look into this on the web. Simply realize that the quickest method to manufacture connects that will check is to use every accessible asset.

Furthermore, as a last note, know this. Try not to be terrified that you may disrupt one the norms of satisfying the crawlers with your connections. You can't generally treat it terribly. By that what is implied is that while the correct blend of connections helps your execution, the 'wrong' blend doesn't extremely hurt it. If you wind up with a connection structure that is too vigorously weighted in one territory, the most exceedingly bad that will apparently happen is that the connections will be marked down, but they won't subtract 'focuses' from your positioning. Generally, they simply wind up impartial. Attempt a couple of things, develop a few connections, and after that go from that point to change your outer connecting.

What Will Work and What You Should Forget About

This is the place we've set this extremely imperative discussion, despite the fact that by a few rights maybe it ought to have come considerably before in the book. At any rate, this is the place we will discuss the watchwords and key expressions that you are to focus on your extremely ready and capable purchasers—the general population who truly need to purchase, that are only a stage before buy, that are spot almost there simply require that last little push!

The best free thing you can do is pick the correct catchphrases that will focus on the correct purchasers. But those watchwords are not what such huge numbers of others have revealed to you require. The enormous push on the web is to get positioned for the most mainstream watchwords. If you achieve that, you'll have so much activity nothing else will matter. There are a couple of things amiss with this strategy and rationale.

- It is too difficult to break into the high rankings for the most famous hunt terms.

- Traffic doesn't make a difference as much as change does.

- Most looked does not equivalent spurred purchaser.

- It disregards the long tail of catchphrases that on the whole means greater and preferred activity over a solitary best watchword.

The most vital factor that we need to consider is that by constructing your catchphrase seeks with respect to what the most famous look terms are for a specialty, you are not specifically focusing on those individuals who are eager, persuaded, on-the-cusp purchasers. You're basically gathering everybody out there with an enthusiasm for gadgets or working out powders, who could be everybody from children inquiring about school papers to individuals who detest gadgets or some real buyers searching for gadgets and enhancements to purchase.

Optional and long-tail catchphrases/phrases are really the movement that you need most. The reason is basic—provided that you make sense of what the persuaded purchasers are utilizing as their pursuit terms, rather than every other person looking into your specialty, you will get rid of the lighten, and simply net in the rush hour gridlock you need. It may not be as noteworthy as acquiring guests by the thousands, but who cares if those guests will probably be purchasers?!

Picking the right—beneficial—catchphrases is less demanding than you might suspect. You simply need to comprehend what purchasers look for. This will differ contingent upon what you are offering, but when in doubt purchasers will search for data about an item before they will simply search for the item. They'll search for the exhortation of others on the web. They'll search for suppositions and data offered in specific sorts of substance like item audits. For these individuals you need to pick watchwords that incorporate things like

- Product x audit

- Product x feeling

- Product x examination

Et cetera.

The issue driven shopper may likewise be searching for an answer. These sorts of purchasers are effortlessly focused with instructional exercises that offer the arrangement they require. With this you have one of two alternatives—either give complex instructional exercises and point to a superior way, or end your instructional exercise with your item, or generally incorporate it as basic to the fix. For these individuals you would need to incorporate watchwords, for example,

- X How to

- How to do x

- Repair issue

- Fix issue

- Problem settle

- Cure

- Clean

- Problems

At this point you should see where we're running with this. The general population who require you are not simply circumventing sitting idle in wide pursuits; they are specifically tending to their necessities and worries with their inquiry terms. Subsequently, what you need to do is give them what they are searching for, and improve utilizing the terms that the general population you truly need visiting are utilizing.

This is the watchword and SEO procedure that you will use for every one of your little, item focused sites. By doing this on numerous sites for different items, you will, after some time, catch a lot of the activity rankings for your specialty all in all. That is the point at which you utilize your parent site to tidy up. On your parent site, you begin upgrading for the greater, more broad watchwords. You would now be able to do this since you have a sufficiently huge connection structure built up outside in the auxiliary catchphrase markets to help the bigger site, and accordingly you've set up enough capacity to rank well with the parent site in brief time. In the long run, the jobs turn around and the parent encourages the littler destinations, but the jobs don't generally make a difference. The only thing that is important to you is that by some turn, the movement is controlled by you.

This is, by a wide margin, a standout amongst the best procedures utilized by the Big Shots. Hotshots love web marketing for its straightforwardness and productivity. They are hoping to profit with restricted yield. So they focus on what will get the most purchasers, generally effectively. What's more, this is it. If you don't take in whatever else from this book, figure out how to focus on a purchasing gathering of people like the Big Shots do. Figure out how to pick the watchwords whereupon everything else will be based, and appreciate higher changes and intrigue essentially as a matter of course.

Making Your Own Products

It's a basic, exceptionally consistent idea—if you can profit as an affiliate, how huge could your income stream be if you were the maker of the item?

You realize that as an affiliate you make x percent of every item sold. Suppose you're acquiring a commission of say half. That implies that you are not making half of the income created from that deal. Somebody is making the same amount of as much as you seem to be! Presently indeed, we'll give you this one point—that somebody is additionally paying the costs of improvement and generation and other overhead, but you can wager they've set their cost at well above costs!

To be clear, we are not prescribing that you attempt to make your own items as opposed to wind up an affiliate. We are prescribing that after you have set up your business as a compelling web advertiser, that you at that point use your impact to advance results of your own and trade out by mesh the greatest piece of your deals. We should speak somewhat about how this should be possible.

The Back-End Sales Effect

What this private item creation procedure depends on is you having effectively settled an a dependable balance in the market, inside your specialty. You've done this by utilizing the methodologies sketched out in this book, by making item engaged sites and after that connecting them together with the parent webpage which catches whatever is left of the general web activity searching for your specialty content. What's more, now that you have everybody's consideration, you can utilize it to up pitch your returning guests to your own items.

What Might You Sell?

Much like the freeware items that helped your activity, you have to offer something that associates with what you've been offering from the start. But you do need to understand that your purchasers won't return in time. You can't simply offer them on something less complex that they may have purchased previously; you need to offer them on something that serves them in their next period of life, or that improves what they've just purchased.

As a rule, this will be something that is carefully created. For example, if you beforehand sold weight training supplements, your next item may be an eBook or lifting weights program that the purchaser pursues to make those enormous muscle gains. If it's the time to get down to business exercise video, possibly the item that you construct is a dietary arrangement or for the time-impeded.

It is significant, as well, while we have this discussion, that you can tackle the intensity of back-end (as in committed, trusting, return purchasers) deals with other affiliate items also. For example, assuming you conclude that being an item designer is only not for you, you can gathering and up offer complimentary items. Moreover, you can likewise invert the procedure a bit with the goal that you are first offering your item—an eBook or something comparably simple to make—and after that up-offer an affiliate item.

Item Development Options

Presumably, most who are getting into affiliate deals are not the individuals who at any point thought they'd build up an item to offer as their own. This may persuade that making your very own item is past you.

In any case, as we stated, we're basically discussing items that are carefully made somehow. We're not really proposing you go out and develop anything substantial. Some item alternatives may include:

- EBooks

- Software programs

- Web Templates

- Applications and modules

- Courses, web based preparing

What's more, this is only the start.

You have a few alternatives regardless of whether you don't really have the ability to make one of these items yourself. Contracting an independent essayist or software engineer is simple, on account of online classified advertisements like Craig's List and independent sites like GetAFreelancer and RentACoder. Since you are as of now profiting, and you will profit with your item, you would now be able to justify the cost. It's only a piece of your item improvement spending plan and strategy for success.

Releasing Affiliate Power

When you have a quality item, your next regular advance will be to do what got you into this entire wreckage—offer your item through ClickBank or another and produce your very own affiliate deals. Your very own extremely settled affiliate deals will turn some incredible benefits for you, but envision now if you combined with affiliates and increase that over the web!? Motivate others to offer your items for you. Do the establishment work, post a few deals and changes worth boasting about, and after that let the intensity of the web deals constrain offer your item for you!

You truly have nothing to lose by building up an affiliate program. If you have an item that is offering admirably, it will offer through other skilled affiliates, as well. Furthermore, since it costs you nothing except if a deal is made, there is literally nothing to lose. It's the excellence of affiliate marketing, and it's the reason this business is so inconceivably famous, and why this is the way online items offer fundamentally—through direct deals and affiliations.

The Beauty of Duplicity

The more beautiful thing about building up your very own item is that you can do it in different varieties over and over, and along these lines profit by the excellence of trickery. Appear to be secretive? It's most certainly not.

The first run through is the hardest time. In this manner, if you can figure out how to make a decent offering item once, you can reproduce and catch more piece of the pie by doing it over and over. You can, as a result, control a greater amount of the piece of the overall industry just by making what appear to contend items.

The excellence of this is you don't need to begin starting with no outside help inevitably. You should simply roll out little improvements and change your unique item, give it another name and area, make another brand, and pursue a similar way to progress. The genuine magnificence is that you turn into an extent of your opposition—relatively dependent on the measure of your specialty advertise and on the occasions you re-make your item.

To catch additionally intensity of trickery, you can likewise make focused items and pitch the rights to them, either in full or Private Label Rights that others can purchase and exchange as their own.

Since you are as yet paid on your end each time the item is sold, despite everything you profit. (Make sure that you find out about and comprehend the different sorts of rights with the goal that you don't unlawfully exchange the item; Private Label Rights, or PLR enables you to exchange a similar item on numerous occasions, though full rights does not. There might be other middle of the road rights choices that you can investigate to get more mileage from your items also.)

The facts confirm that the majority of this variety expands the opposition against your very own items, but for this situation that is surely not a terrible thing. For a certain something, all that it intends to have rivalry is that there is room inside the market to help it. New aggressive items would not (and ought not) be made in a specialty without interest. All the more essentially, you are making your own opposition. At a certain point or another, you are profiting from the item. You are just increasing your wage by making your own opposition.

What's more, after every finishing, you are prepared for the last advance, which duplicates the magnificence of trickery once more, opening the conduits for a close boundless marketing potential. We think you'll perceive this last stage.

Releasing Affiliate Power

Do we rehash ourselves? A tad, but this time, with a curve.

The last stage is the equivalent as the last stage in the marketing of your first self-created item—making a boundless marketing also, deals compel. Envision the intensity of not just making that power for your item, and making and controlling your own opposition, as well as at that point offering those items that you control through more affiliate programs! The outcome is the increased intensity of various affiliate programs, all offering items that you possess. There's for all intents and purposes no closure to the conceivable outcomes; and you should simply do again that which you've done previously.

That is it! You've made it! You've quite recently gotten the hang of all that you have to know to leave the young doggie pen and turn into a Big Shot Super Affiliate. We've recently sketched out a whole procedure here that will work for you to make enormous, pain free income through web marketing. We know you're eager to begin, but before you kept running off to discover huge offering affiliate items and begin constructing your "WEmpire", we think you'll need to investigate part 10 (and we seek you'll stick around after our couple of conclusive comments; please—only a couple of minutes more!?). Part 10 is basic, no hard perusing or overwhelming approach, only straight-forward assets recorded completely to help you on your way. So if you'll humor us, only a couple of more minutes of your time. The time, cash, and exertion you spare will be more than worth those minutes.

Chapter 7

Affiliate Marketing Future Trends and Success Guidelines

How to Make Money In The Future

It is extremely conceivable getting rich doing affiliate marketing disregarding the monstrous rivalry. Despite the fact that Affiliate marketing isn't an income sans work tree that is going to simply drop packs of money into your lap with no exertion on your part required, you can even now make a fortune offering other individuals' items – if you know how to do it right.

You will discover the affiliate openings that work the best just by discovering them yourself, either through testing and look into or systems administration and business improvement.

Free activity isn't totally finished but it is blurring quick. You can strive to make pages that score high in the web search tools and incorporate perspiration value with a website but by paying for snaps and concentrating on Google and Overture you will have the best three positions on all web indexes that truly depend on the Internet.

You should be over if you need to produce activity from Yahoo. Suggestion and particularly Google are the best key drivers of qualified activity on the Internet.

Getting every one of the Tools You Need

The first and most critical instrument an affiliate advertiser must have is his or her own site. The initial phase in any effective affiliate marketing business is building a decent, solid and expert looking site.

Your site is the hopping off purpose of all your marketing endeavors. Assemble an easy to use site, which will pull in your prospects and inspire them to tap on the connections to the items and administrations you are advancing and make a buy.

The second device in your stockpile ought to be offers and motivators. Rivalry is a noteworthy issue in the Internet world.

You should dependably be one-advance in front of your opponents to guarantee that you catch a substantial part of your objective market so you should utilize each conceivable way to rouse people not exclusively to visit your webpage but additionally to snap and continue to the sites of the items and administrations you are advancing.

Building a pick in email list is extraordinary compared to other approaches to assemble prospects. Offer a bulletin or an E-zine. Even better, offer motivations to your prospects to urge them to buy in to your pamphlets. You can show free programming, free online recordings, access to restrictive administrations and different complimentary gifts that will be useful to your prospects.

Your ability and learning is another critical device to use to make your site a well known Internet connect to visit. Outstanding amongst other approaches to do this - at no expense by any means - is by submitting articles, with your site's connection at the asset box, to E-zines and free article locales.

You won't just pick up introduction, you will likewise have the chance to publicize for nothing, simply incorporate a connection back to your site. The more locales you present your articles to, the better your connection prominence moves toward becoming.

The Age-Old Question Do You Need a Website?

The most vital and crucial thing to guarantee your accomplishment in affiliate marketing is your own site. The initial phase in any fruitful affiliate marketing business is building a decent, valid and proficient looking site. Your site is the bounce off purpose of all your marketing endeavors.

Thusly, you should initially fabricate an easy to use site, which will draw in your prospects and propel them to tap on the connections to the items and administrations you are advancing and make a buy. You should initially center your endeavors in building a site that will take into account what your prospects require.

To the exclusion of everything else, make your site brimming with unique, pertinent and valuable substance. The most imperative thing you ought to consider is that all web clients go online to search for data, not really to go and purchase something. Individuals will love articles that are engaging and supportive.

Remember that, in the Internet, content is as yet ruler and great quality substance won't just form your believability, it can likewise enable you to accomplish a higher web crawler positioning. By posting applicable and valuable articles, you build up yourself as a valid master in the field, making you a more reliable endorser of the item or administration you advance.

Setting up a decent name is a decent advance in working up a committed purchaser base. Devoted client bases are the lifeblood of affiliate advertisers.

You should utilize each conceivable means on your site to persuade prospects not exclusively to visit your webpage but likewise to snap and continue to the sites of the items and administrations you are advancing.

When you are making your site, the conceivable outcomes are unfathomable and are restricted just by your creative ability, inventiveness, genius and resolve. You can simply investigate different thoughts and adjust different procedures, which you think may enable you to end up a high moving affiliate advertiser but not until the point when you have an incredible site.

Why an Auto Responder is Your Asset

Automated assistants mechanize the way toward following up email marketing leads. Email Auto responders are extraordinary email tends to that arrival a message or set of messages in light of any email that is sent to the automated assistant's location.

At the point when your business is moderate or simply starting you might be falter to utilize this device on the grounds that the great ones aren't free. But be guaranteed as your business develops, you'll discover an utilization and be happy that you have one.

Most web has have automated assistants – it is just restricted by the quantity of email tends to your host gives you. In any case, there is one little downside to web have automated assistants – you are restricted just to one message for each automated assistant, without the likelihood of a subsequent email to your prospects.

You can buy automated assistant programming. This product can be set on your PC or you can buy an online administration, and all your data will be put away on the server where you obtained the administration.

Automated assistant programming can complete a variety of things to help your affiliate marketing business. Automated assistants can:

- Give planned customers business data, evaluating records and continues

- Collect names and email addresses

- Be utilized for preparing

- Give away free reports

- FAQ (if suitable)

- Auto-send your article entries

It is plain to see there are numerous utilizations, all of which will keep you in contact with your guests or potentially planned leads, and the advancement of your items, administrations and business.

Regardless of whether you utilize a free or paid automated assistant will be specifically controlled by the development of your business – and obviously, your financial plan.

The utilization of automated assistants is just restricted by your creative ability and your morals. Try not to run insane with this apparatus – it is to be utilized to help your business – so know about SPAM – and its customs' – and this instrument will work for you.

Your Main Focus in Affiliate Marketing

The fundamental focal point of all entrepreneurs and their particular Web destinations is site advancement. It isn't something that occurs incidentally, notwithstanding. This is on the grounds that once you have another Web website it requires some investment before web indexes transfer your URL and it turns out to be a piece of query items.

While your Web page may be returned in the consequences of free web crawlers, it will in any case not result in the measure of activity you need but there is one specific approach to build movement to your Web webpage that is cheap, and that is site advancement through bulletins.

Online bulletin editors are searching for new data from new organizations constantly but they more often than not don't have any desire to pay for the article you compose. They like to exchange a byline or a little commercial for your business or site page. Therefore, you should simply spend a couple of hours composing a pamphlet that talks about an important subject and that additionally has a fitting for your website page.

This is a route for you to rapidly get the word out about your site page and additionally increment activity and business while you are sitting tight for the web search tools to get your data in the framework and part of the indexed lists. Pamphlets give simple and free site advancement, so don't disregard the chance.

Try not to exchange the copyright of your article to anybody. Just allow the privilege to print your pamphlet. By doing this, you can present this one pamphlet to numerous E-zines and achieve numerous more potential supporters than you would with just a single.

Likewise, it spares you time since you don't need to compose new pamphlets for each E-zine. When you compose the asset box for your ad, ensure you incorporate your whole site address so people can basically tap on the location and be taken specifically to your page as opposed to cutting and glue. The less demanding you make it, the more people will investigate what you bring to the table.

Accepting Affiliate Payments

The principle issue vendors have with affiliate advertiser installments is that they need to start installments physically dependent on a commission report that would normally be produced by their own e-store programming. If affiliate installments keep running into hundreds or thousands, this procedure can get exceptionally dreary.

Luckily, Paypal (http://www.paypal.com/) has concocted an answer for the dealer's concern. It is called Mass Pay. Basically, Mass Pay is an answer from PayPal that computerizes affiliate installments. Rather than having to physically enter the affiliate sums into the installment framework; their e-store programming creates a Mass Pay document that contains the subtle elements of the installments to be made.

This is a help to affiliate advertisers and extraordinarily decreases the issues related with tolerating installments from vendors. Paypal is the by and large acknowledged approach to get installments from shippers that you have an affiliate marketing concurrences with.

Paypal makes getting installments from people less demanding, also. Having a Paypal button on your site is a genuine aid to you. It makes it straightforward and simple for clients to pay for their buys and is so notable that individuals feel extremely secure utilizing it.

Paypal enables you to set up a business account. It is an exceptionally straightforward process. The main thing you are required to do is give data that enables Paypal to verify your identity and that your financial balances are legitimate. Evidence of a legitimate credit card is additionally a prerequisite. When you have a Paypal business account you can acknowledge charge card installments, too.

You can buy programming that will coordinate with Paypal to help track your affiliate marketing deals and recognize what your bonus is effectively and rapidly. There are a few such programming items available. You can without much of a stretch discover them by utilizing your most loved web index.

Identifying an Existing Hot Demand

Each entrepreneur realizes that opposition is intense, but he or she will most likely be unable to pinpoint precisely what changes are required with the end goal to get to the best. Directing nothing new may never again be adequate.

Putting resources into the innovation that is presently accessible can be an incredible help or a bank breaker. It appears that most private company and locally situated business are either starving (they don't have enough innovation) or they are stout (they have everything bit of new innovation that needs to be addressed).

There is, nonetheless, some genuinely new innovation that each little or domestic venture proprietor needs. It can answer addresses like; by what method can private ventures identify essential patterns, identify a current hot interest and settle on better choices quicker?

Reply: business insight programming. Business knowledge is the precious stone bundle of the 21st century.

Buying business knowledge (BI) programming is a standout amongst the most key speculations that a business can make. Utilizing information mining, revealing and questioning, BI enables organizations to comprehend, screen, oversee and react to specified circumstances.

This product engages leaders — and staff — to come to an obvious conclusion around key business numbers in a way beforehand impossible. BI encourages you make sense of:

- Which clients are gainful?

- Which clients seem gainful but aren't?

- Are you near — or a long way from — achieving basic points of reference?

- When is the best time to dispatch a marketing effort?

- What was the best performing item or administration last quarter?

Business Intelligence programming might be a greater amount of a speculation than independent ventures can shoulder. It can surely be pricy. Private venture or household undertaking proprietors, be that as it may, it can buy in to BI benefits on the Internet at a genuinely sensible expense. There are a few to look over. eBay likewise distributed a "Hot Items" list the main seven day stretch of every month. It gives profitable data to eBay dealers who utilize drop shippers.

Choosing the Right Product

When you first begin your online business, the first and most evident inquiry you will ask yourself is... what am I going to offer? Focuses to consider when choosing the response to that inquiry are:

- Is it light and simple to deliver?

- Is it a computerized decent that is downloaded (E-book or programming)?

- Is it transient or delicate?

- Does it must be seen and held (creator textures, maybe)

- Is there enough interest to make your endeavor gainful?

- Does it have little rivalry from vast online organizations (specialty items)?

The last two qualities are the ones that can be difficult to bind. Here is a for the most part acknowledged strategy for landing at a thought of how overwhelming the interest and rivalry is for an item.

If you have a unique enthusiasm for a few items that meet the above criteria, extraordinary, but don't constrain your examination just to things you like. You are searching for a specialty item with moderately great interest (enough to make it productive), but without overwhelming rivalry.

One approach to perceive what the interest is for items you are occupied with is to take a gander at web crawlers to perceive how as often as possible individuals look for the item you are thinking about.

The aftereffect of this examination ought to be that at least one items will fit into a specialty advertise - items with some interest, and generally little supply. For the best outcomes, center around one specialty item classification, and offer a wide determination. That way, you can turn into the best online hotspot for that specific classification.

For instance, rather than offering general art supplies, offer the most stretched out conceivable choice of needlepoint units. This procedure will likewise enable you to rank higher in web crawlers since you can upgrade your pages for less, more specific, watchwords.

Where to Look for the Right Product Online

When you are simply beginning your online business finding the correct items to offer online is the main issue. Knowing where to look can help.

1. Drop Shipper Directories Drop shippers are wholesalers that will dispatch direct to your clients with the goal that you don't need to put resources into or store stock. Registries of drop shippers are available to be purchased on the web, but ensure you're purchasing a trustworthy one.

2. Local Businesses: You may discover organizations in your terrace that offer only the correct items, but are not yet into E-trade. Offer to offer their item online in return for a level of any benefits you make.

3. Crafters: Local crafters are a decent wellspring of novel items, and might will lessen their costs for you if you buy in amount. Either purchase the thing by and large, or set up a transfer game plan with them.

4. Garage deals and insect markets: G carport deals are a decent place to search for things to offer on the web. Do some investigation into classifications that premium you, and after that begin scouring deals at great costs.

5. eBay: eBay itself can be a hotspot for items. Search for discount parcels that can be separated for individual deal.

6. Wholesaler Directories: Your neighborhood library will most likely have catalogs of makers, wholesalers, as well as distributors. Most indexes are sorted out by SIC code with the goal that you can focus in on the item classes that intrigued you.

7. Trade Shows: Trade demonstrates are an extraordinary method to source items. Bunches of shippers accumulate in one place to search for affiliates. To discover expos in a specific industry, contact exchange affiliations and industry distributions.

8. Importers/Exporters: You should need to consider reaching organizations that import merchandise from abroad. It's conceivable to source specifically from abroad. This requires a great deal of ability, but numerous organizations do it effectively.

How to utilize Auto Responders for Maximum Benefits

In light of the objective of productivity, the most essential inquiry a site proprietor must deliver is the means by which to expand the estimation of guests once you motivate them to visit the site. One critical component of the technique is to make utilization of an automated assistant.

A standout amongst other marketing instruments on the Internet is the automated assistant. This broadly utilized marketing instrument reacts consequently to any email message sent to it.

They are activated by a clear email sent to the automated assistant email address.

For instance, when somebody sends an email to an automated assistant, the individual gets an effectively arranged email message with the asked for data.

This happens naturally and promptly, contingent upon the Internet and email servers.

If you have appropriately set up pick in addition to an automated assistant arrangement, you aren't actually associated with development. The automated assistant contacts the prospect with the underlying answer and past, getting to be essentially you're continually at work, mechanized deals constrain. You should simply set it up one time.

Compose the subsequent messages, program the interims at which you need your messages sent, at that point the automated assistant set-up works for you over and over on autopilot.

Continuously remember that the guest isn't keen on your goals. They just need to recognize how might this benefit them. They've given their email address for the most part since they need to get data, not all that they can peruse your ads.

So give them what they need: exact and valuable data on a specific subject. Procure their trust. At that point, you can tell about how your items and administrations could profit them.

If you don't give great substance, prospects won't continue opening the messages in your arrangement. Make it a win-win. They get great data and you get an all around qualified prospect on account of your automated assistant messages.

Have a Mailing List of Your Own

Regardless of what kind of email you convey, you'll require a mailing list. The fundamental method to assemble a mailing list is by catching name and email address data for everybody who purchases or shows enthusiasm for your item.

An email list that YOU COLLECT YOURSELF is extremely valuable. This can be proficient by utilizing a rundown chief on your site. Rundown supervisors additionally give the HTML coding to the shape on the Gateway pages.

A rundown chief gathers the email tends to that are accumulated with the frame. Subsequently, your email list is gathered. This may take some time so there are techniques to use until the point when you get your own email list assembled.

One approach to assemble a mailing list is to do advertisement swaps with other rundown proprietors. The manner in which this works is, you (as organization A) have an email list that you send pamphlets to and another rundown proprietor (organization B) has a rundown they send bulletins to. Organization An and Company B put promotions on each other's mailing records. Every one of you is advancing the other's rundown.

You can lease or purchase focused on email records. The rundown you create utilizing your own clients' names is called your "home rundown." obviously, when you're first beginning, your home rundown is probably going to be scanty. To increase it, one approach is lease or purchase a mailing list.

There are two different ways to purchase or lease a mailing list—moving toward the organization you need to lease from specifically or utilizing a rundown dealer. Any organization that messages data to its clients for the most part has a rundown chief, who handles request and requests for the mailing list.

Another approach to fabricate an email list is to list your bulletin in the majority of the E-zine indexes.

Have Your Own Voice through Creating Special Reports

You're most likely hunting down extra income streams to keep your business strong and secure in this contracting economy and unverifiable world. Creating particular substance available to be purchased is one of the quickest, most solid techniques for making additional salary quick.

Composing a "white paper" or an extraordinary report, is an incredible method to set yourself up as a specialist in your field, and offer important data with your prospects.

You may as of now have the greater part of the elements for an E-book or uncommon report in your records or files. Discover which fixings make clients willing to pay you for material accessible from different sources, and what components you ought to incorporate into your marketing duplicate to start their enthusiasm for purchasing now.

Here are the means to take when composing your unique report:

- Have your true objective at the top of the priority list before you begin.

- Do you need to figure out how to build deals, while decreasing your expense to get those deals?

- Who would you say you are attempting to awe and what is critical to them?

- What distribution technique will be ideal?

- How numerous individuals would you like to affect with this report?

- Make beyond any doubt the design of your extraordinary report looks satisfying, and is anything but difficult to peruse.

- Keep as a main priority that it's essentially persuasiveness in print.

- Keep your actualities precise, exceptionally concise and to the point. The denser your data, the more profitable and more inclined to keep the enthusiasm of your peruser.

- Write an eye-catching feature. 95% of your perusers will choose if they will peruse your uncommon report dependent on your feature, so make it extraordinary and make it advantage driven.

Get it on the web. While messaging others, incorporate your white paper URL in your SIG line of your Email or incorporate the URL while advancing your unique write about Email talk records.

Setting up your Affiliate Marketing System

There is much theory about how much cash you can gain online without your very own item. Marketing your very own advanced item on the Internet can be extremely lucrative but there is no motivation behind why you can't benefit a lot by utilizing imaginative strategies that offer genuine incentive to Internet surfers and have your very own item too.

An affiliate program is truly not as difficult to set up as you may think. Because of the popularity for affiliate frameworks as of late, there are currently heaps of approaches to set up your very own program.

This is what you have to set one up:

1. A site with your very own area name.

2. At minimum one item or administration that you possess totally.

3. A framework to deal with commission following and installment.

That sounds truly simple, isn't that right? Indeed, really it is! Furthermore, it's getting simpler constantly.

The initial two things recorded above are clear as crystal. Obviously, you require your own site and your own item or administration. You can't set up a partner program if you don't possess the site or the product(s) you will advance.

If you have not made these two strides, you'll have to do them first. Once you've figured out how to get by these two stages, you can move appropriate to stage three, setting up your program.

You should look the Internet for a framework that will deal with commission following and installment. You can endeavor to do this without anyone's help but you will in all likelihood miss a few and missed ones are missed salary. There are free ones, and additionally, paid ones.

The positive parts of a partner administration framework are many.

1. You can sign on partners all the more quickly and grow a bigger power of affiliates.

2. You'll appreciate the mechanization and online administration of affiliates.

3.   These frameworks give full deals measurements to both you and your partners.

How to Get Targeted Traffic

You have manufactured an extraordinary site and have a great deal of affiliates but you simply don't have enough movement... not sufficiently near activity... on your site. What can you to do expand the activity... the TARGETED movement? As a matter of fact, there are a few things that you can do that will help.

1.   SEO (Search Engine Optimization) ought to be your objective! The principle wellspring of activity to any site is the web crawlers. The most utilized web search tools are Google, trailed by MSN and Yahoo. You should upgrade your site for the web crawlers. This incorporates off/site joins and/on hand strategies.

2.   Article marketing is a standout amongst the best approaches to get focused on guests to your site. Getting your articles distributed in E-zines and on chose and related locales will produce a gigantic measure of activity to your site. Try to compose supportive how-to articles on current subjects that different website admins need on their destinations. This will support your connection prominence with the web crawlers and increment your rankings. You should likewise painstakingly pick the correct catchphrases to focus in your articles, coordinating the substance on your site. You should target catchphrases that have high movement, yet little rivalry from contending sites.

3.   Viral marketing procedures work. One viral strategy to pull in focused guests is to offer a free item or administration. Pick items that can be marked with your connections and go around. Supportive programming programs that match the subject of your site are great decisions to make.

4.   Blogs and RSS (Real Simple Syndication) channels are another approach to successfully increment focused on activity to your site. Make basic web journals and channels for the real themes of your webpage: on rss assets, web facilitating arrangements, note pad PCs, and so on. These web journals and feeds acquire an extraordinary number of focused guests.

Using Pay-Per-Click

The two best pay-per-click web search tools are Google and Yahoo, there are, be that as it may, others. Pay-per-click web crawlers enable organizations to offer on watchwords that identify with their locales. Organizations present their site's depictions and titles, alongside a rundown of catchphrases to the motor. They likewise specify the measure of cash that they're willing to spend on every watchword.

After a compensation for every snap web index forms the organization's demand, their outcomes begin showing up when somebody scans for a catchphrase that the organization paid for. Contingent on how much cash others paid rankings for a specific watchword perhaps high or low.

Pay-per-click promoters pay just when their advertisement is tapped on from query items (navigate). Most motors specify a base measure of cash required for an organization to open a record.

Numerous individuals feel that paid rankings diminish the pertinence of indexed lists by enabling any site with cash to rank high for any catchphrase. Pay-per-click motors comprehend that they will lose searchers, and in the end publicists, with superfluous outcomes, and in this manner, make pertinence a need.

Notwithstanding, pay-per-click motors will give results business, not instructive data. Significance doesn't ensure the nature of the site. That is the reason pay-per-click motors use editors to audit approaching solicitations for offering. These editors are in charge of ensuring that the submitted watchwords identify with the site's substance.

Individuals get over the top about their watchwords. This isn't right. It is difficult if not difficult to get high rankings dependent on catchphrases. Rather, you have to consider key expressions.

The most effortless approach to do this is to ask yourself "What might somebody endeavoring to discover me compose in when they look?" Make a rundown of these. Give them a shot on the web crawlers - put on a show to be somebody searching for your item or administration.

Purchasing Domain Names

All new site adventures online incorporate an area name. Some of the time the area is obtained from a space intermediary - somebody who has practical experience in exchanging area names.

More often than not, in any case, it will be enrolled through a space enlistment center, for example, GoDaddy or venuecom. Regardless of how it is bought, in all cases, the space name (or names) for a site ought to be precisely considered. The premise of the marketing for the site will be the area name picked.

There are four essential strides to pursue to guarantee an attractive name for your site. While picking and enlisting a space name for another site, tail them each time and you'll have effective areas without fail.

Step #1: Choose a name. Picking a name might be as simple as "your business name website" or it might be more difficult (particularly if you have a typical name for your business). In all cases, your business' name ought to be your main pick for your area name. If your business name is difficult to spell effortlessly, endeavor to enroll incorrect spellings of it too.

Step #2: Make a rundown of words or short expressions that have something to do with your business. Six to ten of these regard begin. When you have the rundown, evacuate the majority of the ones that have in excess of twenty characters in them (this keeps them short). At that point make new augmentations to your rundown by supplanting void spaces with "- " and "_" characters. At last, pack the dispersed words into single word.

Step #3: Check for space accessibility. Go to any area recorder and enter the spaces in the request they are numbered on your rundown. Cross out any names on your rundowns that aren't accessible. When you're done, you ought to have a short rundown of accessible, great areas for your business.

Step #4: Register your space. Space recorders are everywhere throughout the Web with changing costs and administrations. A decent recorder merits any additional cash that might be spent since an enlistment center leaving business could undoubtedly cause cerebral pains and bad dreams for you.

Driving Traffic with Blogs

A great many people who perform seeks utilizing web crawlers are really searching for data as well as for arrangements. The more supportive and pertinent the substance you have on your site blog, the less demanding it is for you to pull in guests and furthermore to transform them into faithful perusers and endorsers. If your blog has significant substance, this will draw in perusers to your blog who will visit once more.

With a Blog, you can submit to the many Blog catalogs that exist on the web. By submitting to blog indexes in the correct classification, you can grow your range to focused supporters or perusers who need to peruse what you're posting on your territory of specialization.

Web journals advance relationship building and trust with your perusers since it enables you to associate with them. Your perusers can allude a companion and envision the activity control that can be created if every single one of your perusers makes a referral. For instance, if you have 1000 perusers and every one makes a referral, that will be an extra 1000 new endorsers, giving you an aggregate of 2,000 supporters/perusers.

Online journals will enable you to construct activity by pulling in web crawler 'bot's to visit the website all the more regularly. All web indexes have a program known as an 'internet searcher bot' which essentially 'insects' or hunts sites and reclaim the outcomes they have to the web crawlers.

Also, 'web crawler bots' adoration content, particularly pages with related watchwords. The more much of the time you refresh your pages, the more every now and again that web crawlers will insect your webpage.

A Blog is really a substance administration framework. If that sounds excessively specialized, a Blog is a push-button distributing framework. Not at all like site pages there is no transferring of pages to web have accounts. Blog postings are in a flash distributed and are consequently facilitated for you. The facilitating is additionally free incidentally.

Art of Paid Advertising

To profit all that truly matters is marketing. You needn't bother with a superior item or a lower cost to profit than your opposition. Actually you can truly make millions offering average items - if you know how to showcase them adequately.

Obviously, you ought to dependably endeavor to convey quality items and extraordinary incentive to your clients - but the fact of the matter is that marketing is all that truly matters.

It's what you should burn through at least 90% of your time doing if you have any expectations of building up a gainful online business. Doing printed material, building sites, noting email, and handling orders doesn't help develop your business - just promoting does.

There are extremely only two sorts of promoting - that which you pay for and that which you get for nothing. Also, both ought to have their place in your general marketing methodology.

Viable "free promoting" procedures do exist, be that as it may, most importantly there are just 24 hours in multi day and there's just so much you can do amid that time. Free promoting methodologies can be viable, but ordinarily, anything that is free will cost you time.

Capitalizing on paid for publicizing and getting it without a ton of venture of time is the question. If you could burn through $1,000 every day on publicizing to make $1,500 per day in benefits - without investing hours doing it - for what reason wouldn't you simply do that? It's not hard by any means. Consider Google Adwords for instance, where you can purchase navigate advertisements for as meager as 1-25 pennies.

That fits the recipe pleasantly. Google alone won't send you enough activity to make you rich, but it's a decent case of viably advancing your site without investing much energy doing it. There are bunches of others.

Your Mailing List and Effective Email Marketing

There is an email marketing system which not very many Internet organizations utilize and utilize legitimately. It's classified "select in arrangement email marketing." This is a mystery weapon a large number of the huge name advertisers incline toward not to discuss much.

It works this way: You offer an alluring and compelling complimentary gift at your site, (much of the time this works best through a spring up or fly under) and when your guests guarantee their complimentary gift, they are required to enter their name and email address.

They at that point are bought in to your arrangement of customized, planned email messages that you have pre-composed. The best sort of arrangement is one that offers free profitable help and data about the subject they were searching for help on in any case.

An elegantly composed email arrangement will frame associations with your best prospects, something that holds more an incentive than most online organizations figure it out. The best piece of this procedure is that once you do the setup work, everything is totally computerized and customized. There are various destinations that offer follow-up email automated assistant administrations.

You can utilize your pick in email rundown to convey bulletins. Bulletins ought to dependably be loaded up with accommodating and current data and ought to likewise incorporate complimentary gifts to guarantee they will be perused. It's a given that connects to your site ought to be conspicuously shown.

Until the point when you get your own select in email list worked there is dependably email bulletin arrange promoting you can consider. More or less, you pay email bulletin administration destinations to run top sponsorship advertisements over their system of pamphlets.

The activity can be focused to pretty much any specialty and it's quicker that discovering E-zines yourself. In spite of the fact that this requires a bigger introductory venture than running promotions in individual E-zines, over the long haul it is generally less expensive and it requires considerably less exertion.

Other Effective Affiliate Marketing Methods

Most affiliate advertisers, even new ones, are exceptionally very much aware of and utilize the conspicuous instruments to showcase their items like Google Adwords, messages, online journals, and composing articles for E-zines. There are no less than three other successful strategies for affiliate marketing that are not exactly so self-evident.

•	Offering coupons as impetuses has for some time been a physical business apparatus utilized for getting customers into stores. It can likewise be utilized on the Internet. With near 80% of customers utilizing coupons, covering all the real age gatherings, it can mean one intense marketing device. Coupons can be an extremely successful device in achieving your focused on market portion and offering your items. One each business should investigate and check whether it's proper for their items. Coupons can be utilized as a minimal effort method for bringing your item into the commercial center. Giving out free examples or markdown coupons can accumulate faithful clients who first attempt your item for nothing or at a reduced rate. Building brand dedication is the one of the signs of a building up a effective item or administration. Utilizing coupons is one strategy for bringing your clients back for additional, over and over. After some time, your items will pick up the trust of the purchaser.

•	Regular posting on major online gatherings isn't an undeniable method to direct people to your site but it works. You should pursue every one of the principles of any discussion and most refuse conspicuous publicizing but by posting consistently you can work your promotions in and since individuals purchase from those they trust, your deals will be expanded by a bigger percent than your movement.

• Use free brand-capable reports that guests can download and utilize. These reports and E-books ought to have interfaces back to your site (or destinations).

Act of Spamming

The word reference characterizes Spamming as the sending of spontaneous mass email - that is, email that was not requested (spontaneous) and gotten by different beneficiaries (mass). A further normal meaning of SPAM confines it to spontaneous business email, a definition that does not consider non-business requesting, for example, political or religious pitches, regardless of whether spontaneous, as SPAM.

SPAMmers have built up an assortment of Spamming strategies, which change by media: email SPAM, texting SPAM, Usenet newsgroup SPAM, web index SPAM, SPAM in sites, and cell phone informing SPAM.

The CAN-SPAM Act (ordered in 2003) applies to basically all organizations in the US that utilization email. It characterizes a "business electronic mail message" - or, in other words this law - as any email message "the basic role of which is the business ad or advancement of a business item or administration (counting content on an Internet site worked for a business reason)" The punishments for glaring Spamming can be serious.

To conform to the counter Spamming law ensure your withdraw framework works. Even better, enable individuals to choose what sorts of messages they wish to get from you. That way you may keep a few people that would quit altogether if they didn't have a decision.

Utilize an affirmed or twofold pick in framework. It is the main way you'll have the capacity to demonstrate that individuals gave express agree to get your email. Indeed, you may lose 30% of your new supporters who never affirm. But they weren't probably going to be great clients in any case. Do what needs to be done and initiate an affirmed pick in framework so you'll be on the ball. Be straightforward in they way you acquire email addresses and in your email advancements.

Trustworthiness is simply great business, obviously, since it demonstrates regard for the client. Business is tied in with addressing client needs - not deceiving them!

Telling Good Traffic from Bad

Regular that passes by you can wager that any genuine site proprietor is thinking about how to get more activity to their site. This extreme want to produce more snaps makes for all intents and purposes any online business visionary simple prey to huge numbers of the activity plans and tricks that plague the Internet.

Wild guarantees of high volume movement and truckloads of money frequently separate even the savviest businessman from their cash since they need to trust the guarantees made by these activity peddlers. The issue is that high volume doesn't really convert into a high deals rate.

The guests who go to your site because of a craving to discover more on a specific, specialty point, not because of leave movement or participation in a protected rundown where individuals just pitch one another.

Great activity originates from individuals clicking joins on points focused to their interests and getting coordinated to a site containing data they need and expect because of tapping the connection. Basically when you get directly down to it the best and most tried and true wellsprings of focused activity originate from connections that individuals click.

Having the capacity to figure out which clicks really result in deals is essential. To track transformations from snap to deals, contingent upon the sort of shopping basket programming you are utilizing, you would then be able to make a custom request affirmation page - i.e. the page that is shown once the exchange is finished. This is anything but difficult to do if you're utilizing an installment preparing administration, for example, PayPal.

It's notable that each web crawler and each site has a specific kind of client (age, interests and so on.), and they'll all have different triggers driving them to buy. These things are critical for you to know with the goal that your publicizing dollars will be spent in the most favorable spots.

Choosing the Wrong Products

Picking what you believe is a hot thing as opposed to picking what premiums you is, as a result, picking the wrong item for affiliate marketing. Investigate any super affiliate and I promise you will see one ongoing idea. They are really intrigued by what they are offering.

Pick items and administrations that interest to you. At that point, do some examination and see whether they are sought after. If they are, locate an appropriate affiliate program and go along with it.

Affiliate marketing is about trust. You have to truly have confidence in the item or administration that you are offering and you, additionally, need to look at it before you advertise it. I you will put your suggestion on something it should be worth each and every penny the proprietor of the item/benefit is inquiring. If not, at that point you have let down the general population you have alluded to the site.

Purchase the item or administration before you join as an affiliate and check whether in truth it conveys what is guaranteed. Research the proprietor of the site, make inquiries, and be meddlesome. After all you will be bringing them business. They ought to have the capacity to answer every one of your inquiries.

Try not to pick items that compensation incredibly low commissions. Many affiliate programs offer peanuts with regards to commissions. 1-2% is just an affront. You will work a similar measure of time and put in a similar measure of exertion to offer 100 items at 2% commission as you would to offer 100 items at 30% commission. Why dupe yourself?

Point of fact affiliate marketing is getting to be a standout amongst the most intense and moderate approaches to procure an exceptionally solid living on the web but you won't acquire that great living except if you have an item that you trust in, one that you know a ton about and one that pays a nice commission on deals.

Unable to Identify a Demand

There is dependably an interest for merchandise and ventures of each kind. You will most likely be unable to identify how expansive or little the interest is but there is in every case SOME interest. Request is the amount requested of a decent or benefit that shoppers intend to purchase in a given timeframe.

Requests are different from needs. Needs are the boundless wants or wishes that individuals have from merchandise or administrations. How often have you felt that you might want something if no one but you could bear the cost of it or if it weren't so costly? Shortage ensures that many - maybe most - of our needs will never be fulfilled.

Request mirrors a choice about which needs to fulfill. If you request something, at that point you've made an arrangement to get it. The amount requested is estimated as a sum for every unit of time. For instance, assume a man expends some espresso daily.

The amount of espresso requested by that individual can be communicated as one glass for every day or seven containers for each week or 365 mugs for every year. Without a period measurement we can't tell whether a specific amount requested is huge or little.

A littler but drawn out interest for a decent or administration might be desirable over a vast and prompt interest since it will be maintained as opposed to here today and gone tomorrow.

When you are hunting down merchandise and ventures for your affiliate marketing business, it is smarter to search for delayed interest rather that quick interest. Taking a gander at crude interest numbers can be beguiling.

Benefit depends on something other than interest. Benefit is controlled by how much commission you are making on every deal. A $50 commission on 100 things is as much as a $1 commission on 5000 things. In this way request isn't all that matters.

Other Notable Common Affiliate Marketing Mistakes

It isn't difficult to set up a decent site and begin and affiliate marketing vocation. It isn't hard at all to discover affiliate marketing openings on the web. In any case, it is an exceptionally straightforward thing to commit dangerous errors that will guarantee your inability to flourish at affiliate marketing.

A standout amongst the most striking affiliate marketing botches is to feel that you should simply locate the ones that compensation the most, join, direct people to that site through your affiliate interface and you're good to go right? Not actually.

It's extraordinary to pick an affiliate program that pays a high rate, but that is not most imperative interesting point. It's substantially more imperative to locate a quality affiliate program that meets certain criteria. Here are three slip-ups you don't need to make:

• You need to ensure the item is a demonstrated vender. You would prefer not to squander your time and cash directing people to a site that doesn't change over. Discover one with a decent transformation rate.

• Make beyond any doubt the site you turn into an affiliate for secures its affiliates, and has your best enthusiasm on a fundamental level. Search for one that gives pennants, messages, and different apparatuses you can use to advance the site. Likewise, ensure that there is just a single installment alternative. As an affiliate advertiser, you should make certain that you will get acknowledgment for your referral. If there is in excess of one installment technique, you can get scammed.

• Do not pick an affiliate program that advances an email course. Nothing is more regrettable than turning into an affiliate to a site that is first objective is to catch email locations, and after that endeavors to make the deal second. As an affiliate advertiser, you have to catch email addresses, at that point to change over that prospect into a deal. Stay with affiliate programs that aren't centered around catching leads since it's just not to your greatest advantage. Construct your own rundown, not somebody else's.

Making Back-End and Residual Commissions

Remaining wage places cash in an affiliate advertiser's pocket with no work or exertion on their part. It doesn't beat that. Offers of back-final results enable you to get paid for work that you accomplish more than once. The thought here is to work more brilliant... not harder.

So what are back-finished results? They are items/administrations you offer to existing clients, i.e. to individuals who have just purchased a first item (front-final result. lead item) from you.

Most online advertisers make considerably more cash offering clients the second, third, fourth and so on item than offering their first item. The reason is that individuals who've just purchased from you once are considerably more prone to purchase once more.

Systems like back-end offers shifts the concentration from the limited "take the cash and run" technique that is such a great amount being used on the Internet today. You've seen these locales everywhere.

The emphasis is on getting an enormous measure of movement and afterward offering guests an over-evaluated item that doesn't convey what was guaranteed. They may profit in the short run but they will just pitch to every client once and should keep spending a great deal of cash on promoting to get new suckers to visit their site.

More fruitful destinations center around building a solid association with their clients. Your fundamental objective shouldn't be to simply ensure your clients are to some degree satisfied...you need them to be to a great degree fulfilled. If you convey the merchandise, your clients will confide in you more.

If you have their trust, you can offer them anything. When you send your extremely fulfilled clients an email offering another item that they would be occupied with, they will run to your site to get it since they trust you. Trust is everything.

Age-Old Question Do You Need to Have Your Own Product

Regardless of whether you need your very own item to wind up a fruitful affiliate advertiser is an inquiry that has been asked and addressed like clockwork since affiliate marketing went ahead the scene. The reason it is asked so regularly is on the grounds that everyone has a different answer.

There are the individuals who say you completely MUST have your very own item to begin and to prevail in affiliate marketing and afterward there are the individuals who say you needn't bother with an item when you begin or ever to be fruitful. Things being what they are, or, in other words? Truly? No?

The truth is that everyone is correct. Having your very own item is extraordinary but it isn't totally important. The individuals who have their very own item can manufacture a site around that item and add affiliate connects to it. The individuals who don't have their very own items can in any case make an extraordinary site and be an affiliate advertiser.

Makers of items love affiliate advertisers and items are not in any way shape or form hard to discover.

The thing that both the individuals who do and the individuals who don't share their very own item have for all intents and purpose is that they both must be enthusiastic about the items they offer. You will never be fruitful in offering something that you aren't keen on yourself.

It takes drive and desire to prevail at any undertaking and affiliate marketing isn't any different. You should be energetic about an item or a thought with the end goal to keep your drive and desire perfectly healthy for the whole deal.

Regardless of whether you are marketing your very own item or an item delivered by others your prosperity is straightforwardly identified with how successful your marketing strategies are, the manner by which centered you are, the way well you deal with your time, and the amount you trust in the item.

Protecting Your Commissions

Cheats are an issue out in the physical world is for entrepreneurs and criminals are a worry for the internet entrepreneurs. Out in the physical world, cheats will take cash and stock and it isn't any different on the web.

This present reality shippers utilize bolts and cautions to deflect cheats. Web entrepreneurs need to utilize against burglary programming to ensure their bonuses. Here are a few things you can do to secure yourself and your bonuses:

1. Use Meta Refresh: A Meta revive is a straightforward piece of HTML code which consequently diverts your guest to another page (your affiliate URL). It gives a slick method for exhibiting affiliate interfaces in bulletins. It presumably diminishes commission bypassing and commission commandeering. A major favorable position of utilizing Meta invigorates is that if shippers change their affiliate joins, you can change connects on many pages rapidly and effectively by modifying just a single record.

One issue is that some web crawlers don't care for meta invigorates in light of the fact that they're every now and again utilized for unpalatable purposes. So if you utilize this system, utilize it with alert.

2. Use a URL redirection benefit. You can utilize free administrations or purchase a remarkable space name for each affiliate program you join. URL redirection makes affiliate connects more subtle, so this will diminish some commission burglaries.

3. Use an online promotion following administration. The promotion following connection at first conceals the affiliate interface, decreasing robberies.

4. Use an advertisement following content. Great advertisement following contents conceal the affiliate connect and also being helpful for following. It has the preferred standpoint that it doesn't advance another person's area.

5. Use JavaScript divert. Since this at first conceals the affiliate connect, it ought to diminish commission robberies.

Know that robbery is an issue for online organizations and find a way to ensure your bonuses.

Is Affiliate Marketing for You?

Affiliate marketing offers numerous chances to make cash taking a shot at the Internet. Turning into an affiliate advertiser is an extraordinary method for having your own online business. Regardless of whether you will be effective at it relies upon numerous things but it for the most part relies upon you.

If you are thinking about doing affiliate marketing, you have just idea of all the manners in which that it could enhance your life like; working for yourself, high salary potential and low activity costs… among numerous different things. Like everything else in life, be that as it may, the fallen angel is dependably in the subtle elements.

Working for yourself sounds so great but what sort of manager will you be. Will you be a slave driver who demands that work be done each waking hour including ends of the week and occasions or will you be so laid back that you won't begin work until late evening and be disorganized to the point that nothing is refined? Either extraordinary will make you an awful manager.

The high salary potential sounds incredible, too, but the watchword here is POTENTIAL. Potential just implies that the high salary is a plausibility and not a sureness. How high your wage will be is straightforwardly proportionate to the amount you will learn and how hard you will function. Turning into an affiliate advertiser doesn't imply that packs of cash will drop from the sky with no time and exertion on your part.

The low task cost of affiliate marketing is an extremely alluring point for turning into an affiliate advertiser. The facts confirm that it is ease… but that doesn't mean there isn't any expense. You will even now have the majority of the typical everyday costs that must be met while you get your affiliate marketing business turning a benefit. You will have promoting costs, also. You should make certain that you can meet your money related commitments previously you dispatch your business.

Utilizing Clickbank as an Affiliate Marketing Career Launch Pad

As one of the greatest data item commercial centers online Clickbank has ended up being an extraordinary affiliate marketing stage notwithstanding for the amateurs in the exchange. Clickbank bargains in the buy and offer of in excess of 30,000 data items. You can take a shot at Clickbank as either a seller or an affiliate. As an affiliate you will be required to offer the educational items that the sellers have made.

For the theme of dialog nearby we will consider what it takes to be an affiliate advertiser on Clickbank. To begin off you should enlist or join. Much like what occurs in different sites you will be required to pick an ID that you will utilize each time you sign in. with this ID set up you would now be able to get to the Clickbank commercial center and test the items which you can offer. Clickbank have organized the commercial center in classifications of items which makes it simple for you to choose what you feel destined to offer. You can pick a solitary thing or a few.

Having chosen the product(s) the following stage will be to gain a 'Hoplink' that will be utilized to guide forthcoming clients to the applicable merchant deals page. The 'Hoplink' appears as a HTML code which is just created after your client ID is gone into an essential frame. Since every item that you need to offer has its own 'Hoplink' you may wind up with a significant number. Clickbank affiliates more often than not record these hoplinks, deals page connections, and item data for simple reference. To offer the Clickbank items that you have chosen you simply need the hoplinks contribution to the business material.

Being a seller isn't difficult either. You simply need an item and pay a sum to have it recorded on the commercial center. Before the item is sold it must be Clickbank endorsed.

Investigating Why There Is Ease in Starting Affiliate Marketing Ventures

Not at all like numerous different organizations where beginning off is extremely hard affiliate marketing has some reasonable points of interest that have made it exceptionally well known with many yearning on the web business people. This is one of only a handful couple of organizations where you can begin gaining a good pay even for the time being.

Maybe the best preferred standpoint there is to affiliate marketing needs to do with the way that there are prepared items which you can begin offering promptly. We as a whole acknowledge that it is so difficult to think of another item and have it turned out to be effective with the end goal that you make a fair wage from your creation. In affiliate marketing you offer items that you are certain of being fruitful with and the scope of these is substantial and differed.

Many new companies experience serious difficulties with regards to issues of gathering installments after deals are made. Affiliate advertisers are not influenced by this as their affiliate shippers do all the gathering from the clients.

In affiliate marketing every advertiser is given an affiliate site by the shipper for whose benefit the marketing is being finished. These sites are independently signed into with the end goal that all exchanges which are made there are attributed to the affiliate advertiser. It is extremely unlikely that you can be precluded from claiming your duty.

Affiliate marketing is tied in with marketing - period. As an advertiser you are not worried about inventories and stock taking and different complexities of regular organizations like conveyance and delivery. Your errand is simply to offer the item and the dealer at that point accepts accountability for getting the acquired thing to the client.

The span of affiliate marketing is generally noteworthy. You can essentially pitch items to any area on earth gave there is a web association. Dissimilar to traditional organizations where the customer base is limited to a city or a nation affiliate marketing implies that the business exertion is worldwide. With affiliate marketing you don't have to stress over exchange limitations that oversee different nations. A few items particularly the enlightening sort just necessitate that the client has a web association and a PC for downloading purposes.

One favorable position that likewise emerges noticeably needs to do with the Internet itself. The web is available every minute of every day 365 and by augmentation your affiliate marketing site additionally is. Regardless of where you are and paying little respect to the time you can simply expect that somebody some place can give you business.

Article Directories Really Help In Affiliate Marketing

Affiliate advertisers must know about every one of the assets available to them that they can use further bolstering their organizations advantage. Business advantage in this setting alludes to the capacity of the dare to charm itself to both existent and imminent customer base.

Affiliate marketing starts from the decision of item that you need to offer. In the wake of choosing an item and a client specialty the time has come to consider what strategies will be utilized to produce deals page activity. There are a few strategies that can be utilized for this reason including SEO and email marketing. The adaptable affiliate advertiser will anyway look to utilize a free strategy known as article marketing. Through article marketing many affiliate advertisers have possessed the capacity to increase significant movement and charming repaying prizes to boot.

Many affiliate advertisers are taking up article composing and accommodation in awareness of the benefits that can be accumulated from doing as such. Prepared articles are submitted to article catalogs where they are distributed upon their delightful of expressed essentials. It is pleasing that few out of every odd advertiser can be a gifted author particularly when the article requires the addition of specific catchphrases. In either case the affiliate advertiser has a marketing employment to deal with. He or she is in an ideal situation contracting an article author to carry out the activity and after that appreciate the expanded volume of movement for quite a while.

With accommodation catalogs one should comprehend that they are now all around set in web crawlers. This is a tremendous shelter for affiliate advertisers and in light of current circumstances. An article that has been all around arranged as far as watchword addition and thickness will without a doubt be positioned exceedingly which converts into more viewership. With expanded viewership it is likewise extremely plausible that this will be converted into deals.

One thing that must be clear about the composition of these articles is with respect to the substance. The ideal article offers the peruser much looked for data about the item specialty zone and not simply the item as such. This is the data that the peruser will experience and ideally settle on a choice concerning whether the item merits purchasing. Articles that have been put in indexes have asset boxes where data about the affiliate advertiser and the affiliate item deal site interface is embedded. It is essential to make the article points of interest as fascinating as conceivable to guarantee that the peruser goes the distance to the base where the asset box is.

Rules for Creating a Superior Affiliate Marketing Website

Your endeavors as an affiliate advertiser ought to be guided towards drawing in online rush hour gridlock to your site and not the other way around. This is the reason the site you structure for this exertion should hold fast to essential rules that are known to be activity amicable.

Lucidity, understanding and consistence are the essential things that you might want your site to be known for. The guest must have the capacity to instantly have an idea regarding what you have on offer as this will influence him or her to peruse on.

The site you have as a top priority ought to be intended to offer the objective planned demographic. The term 'engaging' can be misjudged to imply that the site ought to be loaded with visual impacts and other like increments. In business, a site that is lumbering to those attempting to get to it doesn't make the coveted progress. It is best to have a site that will establish a decent connection from the beginning. Pick your hues and textual styles admirably and also the tone of dialect utilized. Guarantee that you speak with guests in way that will persuade them to work with you.

Close by the issues of importance as have been made reference to over the site ought to be anything but difficult to utilize. While some level of intricacy is fine contingent upon the items and administrations that are being offered being additional complex isn't prudent. What guests acknowledge most in a site is the nature of substance. This is normal for a portion of the more fruitful sites we have around.

While structuring a site you ought to have the mentality of a client whether he or she is a customary purchaser or a prospect. The site ought to however much as could be expected make the guest's experience charming for whatever that he or she needs to do. Give careful consideration to issues of requesting and thing show. The site ought not contain what you believe is best for the activity – the substance ought to be educated by genuine client notions.

An effective site joins brilliant structure with wonderful route. Route includes the utilization of connections that prompt a site page where wanted substance is to be found. Connections ought to along these lines be very much indicated with the goal that a guest can know where the snap will prompt. Nearby route it is essential that a site is routinely refreshed. Access and download speeds are likewise basic to a site's prevalence.

Before picking any affiliate program you should examine and find the best and influence utilization of the equivalent by advancing them before your rivals to catch wind of them. Right now your rivals begin to understand the current affiliate program, you ought to be now profiting from the following executioner item. The general favorable position of the best affiliate programs is that they assist a person with making more cash on the web.

A few affiliates select the wrong projects to advance which by and large confines their capacity to make a decent pay. Fundamentally there is no specific best affiliate marketing program but what you do all relies upon the business sectors that you get included with. It is very easy to pick the affiliate program in that out of the web marketing an individual will discover a chance to ride on the back of the item dispatch and the promotion that it makes. While experiencing the destinations, for example, Commission Junction among others, generally take a gander at the things that are offering the most and get the best.

Such items as of now have a demonstrated reputation and will empower you have a superior time spent in taking a gander at different points with the end goal to draw in purchasing activity other than investing your energy in testing the new affiliate offers in order to see regardless of whether they will change over as you may anticipate. Much of the time, the affiliate items and administrations offers that are offering the most likewise have the best deals pages as the site proprietor has officially done complete testing to accomplish the best transformation rates he or she requires.

It is in every case best to locate the correct activity and send it somewhere else where you as an individual know your odds of making cash are higher by and large. An affiliate benefits in that he or she is

paid for every single client or customer got past his or her exertion. Whenever a customer buys the administration or item, segment of the benefit got from that specific exchange is credited to the affiliates account. This is stored as a commission. Much of the time, the remuneration sum depends on settled an incentive for each visit or each enlistment. With regards to affiliate marketing, the shipper's benefits on a more extensive place to offer their administrations and merchandise which pulls in a lot of clients along these lines, expanded deals.

Pay Increase Tips For Affiliate Marketers

Affiliate marketing has for quite a while been viewed as a definitive huge wage making vocation and it is this misperception that has extremely rattled numerous fledglings. The truth is that there is no such vocation in presence and if there were then it would have just been outside the field of play for a lot of.

Like every single other vocation and employments affiliate marketing is about diligent work and getting the opportunity to take in the ropes well ordered. This is the mantra that affiliate advertiser learners should live by in light of the fact that the underlying background is a long way from the ruddy picture that has been made of the exchange. In reality numerous individuals have stopped their customary employments and set out on affiliate marketing. While some have fared on extremely well some have been disappointed by the high wage illusion.

In affiliate marketing there is no ensured approach to pursue in order to make the high salary that is wanted by many. The methodology that one affiliate advertiser receives and winds up fruitful with isn't really a similar one that another advertiser will thrive with. Affiliate marketing is a greater amount of an individual methodology since it is you who recognizes what your clients like through the correspondence you share. The methodology that you use in the at first will require some tweaking of sorts with respect to the substances on the ground. The business condition wherever is exceptionally unique and the best individuals are the ones who are prepared to adjust to these progressions by being inventive. It is tied in with understanding the requests and wishes of the movement you experience and afterward offering precisely what suits them.

Affiliate advertisers can't stand to be uninformed about necessary subtle elements like inert sentence structure and SEO. Master information on the utilization of catchphrases and the way in which they work is of embodiment. All these are basic to guaranteeing that web search tools work further bolstering your advantage. Affiliate advertisers once in a while thrive without having their very own sites and web journals. Here the significance of watchword expresses in making content rich data again goes to the fore. Such are the essential things one has to know if great wage is to be made.

Because of the fact that individual exertion checks nothing beats understanding. You learn a great deal more by alluding from those who've been in the field longer. This is another method for saying that industry systems administration ought to likewise be considered important.

Is It Possible To Pocket A Six Figure Income Through Affiliate Marketing?

By and large the ones who claim the sites and come up short on the items or the administrations of their own to advertise, it is dependably a hard errand to gain cash through the web. It is conceivable to offer space for publicizing but you need to draw in a few people to your site. You should pull in enormous rush hour gridlock with the end goal to offer the publicizing space. If you don't do as such, you can't have the capacity to win any cash from anyone to give you a chance to promote their locales. If you are inadequately ready to draw in extensive rush hour gridlock to your site and you don't have merchandise and ventures to offer, your answer is the six figure wage program.

In the six figure salary program, the creator teaches a person on the most proficient method to procure at the very least one thousand dollars for each day yearly. The upside of the six figure salary program is that the writer is prepared to help a person in each move he takes. As a rule, most advertisers want to begin gaining cash from home as low maintenance premise. A large portion of the sites rely upon affiliate marketing to empower them gain a great deal of offers since it is a basic idea.

What affiliate marketing by and large involves is offering of other individuals' merchandise and enterprises for a commission which goes between 5 to 25 percent of the item cost. The mystery is to change over the activity to deals by ensuring that the products and ventures you are marketing alone site focus on your guests and target gathering. You ought to likewise guarantee that your adverts don't look like regular ads. This is so on the grounds that numerous individuals don't set aside their opportunity to focus on the standards that are scattered all finished but they do visit your site for data on what you give.

When you are looking for an item as an affiliate you have to take a gander at a few sites that offer the products and enterprises that are identified with your site's data. The greater part of these sites contain affiliate programs and dependably have a connection that is put on their site including the data on how an individual can join to go along with them as an affiliate. Essentially, affiliate advertisers dependably appreciate the advantage of working for themselves and they work time permitting.

Finding Top Affiliate Marketing Programs

Affiliate marketing programs possess large amounts of the web and if you are in the pursuit of a decent one then you will be spoilt for decision. This is anything but a unimportant insult; there are actually a few a great many alternatives which you can investigate. Similarly as with everything accessible online there are great and terrible choices with regards to affiliate marketing programs. A portion of the projects will work to your advantage and others won't be so useful.

The principle thought that numerous potential affiliate advertisers are extremely worried about is the measure of cash that they remain to pick up from their endeavors. The commissions that these affiliate marketing programs offer is very changed. The most astounding paying projects offer as much as 20 to 25 percent on every item that is sold through an advertiser's connections. For such projects business can be great since they distinctively offer items that are enormously well known over the globe.

The second most essential thought that is utilized as a determination foundation by affiliate advertisers needs to do with the notoriety that the program appreciates. You will not turn out badly with a program that is perceived the world over similar to a market pioneer. Clients then again likewise search for brand names that they perceive. Being an affiliate advertiser on a program like Western Union will undoubtedly be fruitful from the get go simply in view of the worldwide acknowledgment. Pick a program that appreciates numerous positive referrals in light of the fact that the errand of changing over these into deals won't be excessively difficult.

Like the point just made reference to about the altruism related with a specific affiliate marketing program is the thought about the items sold in that. A typical trademark that the vast majority of the best affiliate marketing sites share is the way that they offer items that bear extremely prevalent brand names. Such brand names impart loads of certainty into planned clients and even the officially existing ones. It is certain that these items offer most and an affiliate advertiser who offers such is unquestionably going to win solid returns.

Affiliate marketing programs have different methods for managing their affiliates. An affiliate advertiser will improve working with a program that has lovely acquiring motivators like commissions for item advancement through promotions on the affiliate's site. Conceded that joining a significant number of these affiliate marketing programs is free it won't hurt if you take a stab at doing as such.

Spam Complaints and How to Avoid Them in Affiliate Marketing

The fruitful affiliate advertiser has a generous endorser list that he or she can depend upon for maintained business even in lean occasions. The principles of affiliate marketing manage that to keep up such a rundown there must be correspondence between the two gatherings. The endorsers expect that you will be in customary contact with them by following up on their request and remarks. This correspondence is typically by methods for email. Supporters hesitant spam mail and as an affiliate advertiser you should ensure that you don't get spam grievances from any of your endorsers. Spam is an issue that gives affiliate marketing a downright awful name and you essentially can't enable this to destroy a generally lively endeavor.

There are basic things that you can do to guarantee your business is spam protest free. In the first place you should focus on the believability of the data that you give your clients. Whatever the configuration of data you offer them (this can be sound, video, or kept in touch with) you ought to guarantee that it is authentic and dependable. For a business where you can't more often than not reach your believability is estimated upon the substance you offer. For this issue you can't stand to have indiscriminately arranged material on your site. All that the endorsers read must tell them you are a solid master in the assigned territory.

Clients put their trust in the item or administration you are offering basically on the grounds that you said as much. This announcement may be legitimate but it doesn't at all imply that the clients will simply buy anything. The truth is that the Internet is additionally host to a major number of counterfeit items and not every planned client are simple enough to be influenced into obtaining such. As the affiliate advertiser you are relied upon to have done your statistical surveying admirably ahead of time to abstain from winding up with egg all over. You should by and by vet the items you are offering in order to make an educated proposal to the clients.

Remaining concentrated at work is an issue that is basic to any business not to mention affiliate marketing. With center you will be reliably tenacious even in the most modest of points of interest. Organizations develop with time if the working principles are kept up very. With this at the back of your mind your affiliate marketing adventure won't be a failure.

The Definition of Affiliate Marketing and What It Entails

Expanded business rivalry on a worldwide scale has taken off to phenomenal rates especially over the most recent couple of years. Every single business has an expectation of accomplishing economies of scale and this is for the most part done through a decrease of costs wherever conceivable.

Marketing is the methods by which organizations get their items into the client domain. It is the methods through which planned customers are sharpened about the accessibility of items that they need or which they may require. Marketing is certifiably not a shoddy exertion particularly when you consider the media through which it is finished. Generally numerous organizations have been utilizing the Internet as a marketing medium. Affiliate marketing is one of the structures through which this is done and it has ended up being both shabby and powerful.

In affiliate marketing the concerned business has an affiliate(s) whose work it is to lead clients toward the said business. The business at that point remunerates its affiliates for each customer that was landed on account of the endeavors of the affiliates. A business may have affiliates as administration organizations, affiliate supervisors, and affiliate systems. It is these affiliates who lead web marketing in the interest of the business and in this manner advance the merchandise and enterprises that they offer.

Affiliate advertisers have some picked instruments of exchange that they use in the marketing exertion. A portion of the more typical methods to a great extent utilized in affiliate marketing incorporate Search Engine Optimization (SEO), web search tool marketing, and email marketing.

In the developmental days of this marketing strategy products and ventures were regularly advanced by methods for spam. This has anyway changed to the production of website pages. The pages are enhanced for web index positioning using specialty catchphrases. A streamlined website page will without a doubt prompt more webpage movement and subsequently the administration or item being elevated will be presented to a more prominent group of onlookers. Getting enough activity for a developed site can be entirely testing. It is the SEO systems that are for the most part utilized in guaranteeing that an ever increasing number of individuals are made mindful about the site.

Affiliate marketing is yet to accomplish its maximum capacity but its prominence is on the ascent particularly after the advertisers began shunning utilizing spam. The benefits of affiliate marketing are anyway genuine when you consider the insignificant costs included, the worldwide gathering of people, and the brief timeframe length required to get the word around.

The Effect That Blogging Has On Affiliate Marketing

Before we dive into the low down subtle elements of how blogging influences the affiliate marketing exertion it is important that to comprehend what these two phrasings involve. This is particularly for the individuals who are as yet green in such issues.

Blogging is the activity of utilizing a blog also called a web log. As the last name proposes websites are diary like online discussions where individuals post sections which are then successively requested. Numerous online journals are committed to specific theme classes however there are some on which any point can be talked about.

Affiliate marketing includes the online advancement of the merchandise and ventures created by given business. A business that claims a site needs individuals movement who would then be able to be persuaded to purchase. The affiliate marketing exertion is finished by people for the benefit of the business and these people are named to be 'affiliates'. Affiliates utilize a blend of systems to push the advancement motivation. A portion of these strategies are the utilization of web joins, site improvement, and through systems. Affiliates get pay from the business according to the activity they have coordinated to the site.

Online journals have relentlessly increased much prevalence and both affiliate advertisers and web designers have rushed to exploit this reality. Utilizing web journals as discussions for ad and advancement is a pattern that affiliates are presently grasping notwithstanding the others made reference to beforehand. Web designers have improved things by presenting on the web blog programming that encourages more helpful access to organizations by means of the affiliates. Because of this product 'quack' affiliates whose aims are to cheat and trick would now be able to be blocked. This has significantly improved the believability of affiliate marketing.

Blogging has contributed largy to the achievement of affiliate marketing as a methods for online advancement. Using catchphrases web crawlers are more equipped for driving intrigued individuals to the pertinent sites. Not at all like spamming which is disliked blogging isn't as hostile. A well known blog is visited by a lot of individuals in a brief timeframe length and by so completing an item or administration is advertised to a significant huge group of onlookers. With a crowd of people drawn from everywhere throughout the globe numerous organizations have encountered an upsurge in client volume and obviously primary concerns have definitely moved forward. Affiliate marketing on online journals makes utilization of watchwords to coordinate movement. Recordings and photographs are a portion of the extra methods that are utilized to catch the consideration of planned customers.

The Importance of Mailing Lists in Affiliate Marketing

Mailing records are profitable in a few different ways. The best thing about having a mailing list is that an individual can mechanize a considerable measure of the procedure by the utilization of an automated assistant. This is an administration that is offered on the web and it handles the mailings and the mail records for your sake for a little charge that is paid on a month to month premise.

Alternate administrations incorporate the get reaction and a website admin will likewise give an individual access to frame a basic detail that shows up on his or her site. It ordinarily asks the guests the email address and their names. This empowers a person to allure the guests to join by giving a free report in return for the data. It prompts them to wind up the individuals from your mailing list consequently. The mailing rundown's significance to the advertiser is significant. A few advertisers have a great many names on their mailing records and whenever another item is acquainted with the market, the super advertisers have within track on the business utilizing their capacity to contact their different individuals.

Various individuals appreciate affiliate marketing as a method for acquiring a living or to procure strengthening salary. The affiliate marketing development is anything but a difficult errand to comprehend since it gives an approach to help in profiting from retail items without stocking stock, or handle returns if the customer isn't content with the item or make credit deals to the general population. With regards to affiliate marketing, the business procedure is altogether distant.

At the point when there is no work to be done along the lines of making direct deals, there might be a great deal of work engaged with making people in general mindful of the merchandise and ventures you are elevating to them. There are two different ways by which you can draw out your items to general society. One is by acquiring pay per click promoting on the primary web indexes. You can likewise do this by building a site advancing single or a few items. Research uncovers that flow buyers are probably going to buy in coming days. This is on account of it is very less complex to make a deal to a demonstrated client than to pull in another customer.

The Sure Way to Boost Your Niche Affiliate Marketing Business

Owning a site has turned out to be apparently a standout amongst the best approaches to set up a lively specialty affiliate marketing business. With this reality there are numerous contemplations that maturing affiliate advertisers take to mind and a large portion of these need to do with the obliged spending plans that they stick to. To possess a site you don't need to burn up all available resources – at any rate not until the point that you investigate every one of the alternatives that are in your domain.

Buying a site is a standout amongst the most practical alternatives that specialty affiliate advertisers have available to them. The expenses of getting an instant site in any case, the substances of the occasions are to such an extent that such a benefit can be purchased at cordial costs. In considering the expense of such an obtaining you need to gauge the pertinence of the structure to your marketing exertion. Guarantee that these two perspectives supplement each other even before you begin arranging. The second thought needs to do with the substance on the site. You should guarantee that it is all initially novel – not some negligible duplicate glue work.

Acquiring such a site accompanies extremely convenient points of interest. Right off the bat, value that we are on the whole gifted in different fields. As an affiliate advertiser you will most likely be unable to create a site without anyone else and regardless of whether you do it probably won't be as great as what an expert in the territory can accomplish. The other favorable position you will appreciate is the way that a prepared site will empower you to begin marketing immediately. As an augmentation to what has been said on specialization the site will empower you to do what you excel at – marketing – quickly. An instant site makes sure that your business downtime isn't excessively drawn out.

There are things that you should likewise check for when making such a buy. You ought to be sufficiently proficient to identify a specialty affiliate marketing site that you can receive flawlessly. The substance in the site must be discovered for creativity and here online programming like

Copyscape turns out to be extremely helpful. You can't simply purchase indiscriminately – check the merchant's experience to make sure about his or her believability. The costs that you cause in this undertaking may appear to forbid at the beginning but with a valuable site set up for your clients you will appreciate business as soon as possible.

Composing Quality Keyword Rich Articles for Affiliate Marketing

The utilization of watchwords in article composing is predominantly to achieve top positioning in the different web crawlers. No doubt if watchwords are the way to getting best positioning at that point soaking articles with these expressions would be the triumphant methodology. This isn't the situation since doing as such has been known to result in undesired outcomes after scouring the web crawlers.

The motivation behind why this happens is because of the website admin created calculations which decide those articles that are loaded up with significant substance and those that are definitely not. The training as of now is to have articles whose catchphrase content makes around 12 percent of the aggregate word volume. Articles that are esteemed to have outperformed these stipulations are regularly looked with the danger of being prohibited. Affiliate advertisers who require SEO articles require not stress since there are a lot of skilled scholars over the globe who are fit for embeddings the correct number of watchwords into an article while guaranteeing that the substance is educational and consistent.

The fundamental rules for composing SEO articles along these lines all need to do with how the required expression distribution is finished. A perfect situation is to have a couple of catchphrases in both the beginning and completion sections. Every one of the passages in the middle of these two ought to have somewhere around one catchphrase relying upon the length of the article. This may anyway be very precarious when the coveted watchword is difficult to embed by righteousness of its wording course of action. In such situations article essayists are ordinarily offered the accommodation of utilizing both particular and plural types of the equivalent.

While composing catchphrase rich articles it is prudent to continue perusing the article as it creates and upon its consummation. This is to guarantee that soundness is kept up. The best articles are the ones that keep the peruser drew in through and through in a way that they don't appear to take note the rehashed expressions. Of course it is conceivable that the catchphrases are all around distributed but the center substance isn't enlightening. Such an article may breeze through the calculation test but will unquestionably tumble with the perusers consequently influencing the deals adversely.

Notwithstanding the difficulty that might be available when utilizing catchphrases it will be counterproductive to constrain the expression just anyplace. This influences the entire article as understanding the substance ends up difficult. Again this is a valid justification to employ an expert SEO article author. They do charge some cash but this is effectively recovered from the deals that outcome.

Utilizing Link Building to Market Your Affiliate Website

A few proprietors of online business predominantly the ones who need entire web marketing foundation have an unmistakable marketing plan that getting countless for their sites is a valuable factor. In genuine sense, completing back the connections when wrongly consequently murders the site. There are a few different ways to return the executed connects to a person's online site. Article marketing has extraordinary points of interest over different techniques for third party referencing. Different sites proprietors likewise discover connects by sending their destinations to various connection indexes.

If you have a substantial number of connections on the web, its simply like an assurance for most web crawlers to get your connections and discover their way to your site. Some online entrepreneurs post their connections on discussions and web journals with the end goal to get customers. These discussions are very better methods for building joins. This is so in light of the fact that it enables the entrepreneur to interface and bond with other individuals on the web. Other individuals will see, view and react to the remarks. They can likewise surf on your site and see what you offer on it. The technique can be tedious since it requires excessively investment to post the gatherings and websites. But it likewise requires a ton of investment for other individuals to overlook your online site.

A few people favor article marketing as the best contrasted with different connections in that article advertisers more often than not gives them space to get their marketing over all other third party referencing quick. Through composition great articles, the perusers see them and discover the learning or the data that they should impart to other people.

For them to discover more, they can simply focus on the connections in the bio boxes about the creators and visit the distributer sites.

Aside from quality movement and high rankings, article marketing is additionally profoundly adaptable. There is an incredible aggregate impact the same number of articles continue being submitted and affirmed by the article catalogs. If article composing is completed altogether for about couple of weeks, perusers will peruse and trust the scholars as should be obvious for themselves the devotion endeavors that are generally put by the article advertisers – dependable data is the triumphant exertion. Here an individual currently has a few channels. The article advertisers know how to utilize this technique to give different people a chance to see them as specialists in that specific field.

Utilizing Social Networking to Market Your Affiliate Site

Interpersonal interaction is one of the techniques for affiliate marketing procedures which can assist you with selling more affiliate items and administrations on the web. The affiliate business based at home can be utilized to pick up an assortment of best affiliate marketing systems which are generally utilized on the web. Site advancement, standard commercials, web crawlers and email marketing among others are altogether founded on affiliate marketing business however there are organizing sites which can likewise be taken as part procedures for the locally established affiliate business.

Interpersonal interaction is the least expensive and easiest locally established affiliate marketing business methodology choice that is promptly accessible. Publicizing your locally established affiliate marketing business is another best affiliate marketing system on the web that can be run effectively. Long range interpersonal communication destinations are basically online spots when you can meet with your customers. For the most part, most long range interpersonal communication sites depend on specific subjects and they energize the individuals who share same interests in specific points with the end goal to get together to talk about the important issues, give guidance and make inquiries among others.

These long range interpersonal communication destinations can center around any subject. They can likewise center around subjects, for example, legislative issues, TV programs, groups, occupations, recent developments, and leisure activities or insect conceivable theme. The affiliate advertiser can exploit the person to person communication site with the end goal to achieve an intended interest group without burning through cash. Working at home has turned out to be progressively famous and there are various sites which center around this specific subject. There are additionally a few systems administration locales which are engaged and committed to the theme of working at home. Here the gatherings who are keen on this specific subject can take the locally situated affiliate marketing opportunity with the end goal to present a connection on his site when it offers a profitable thing to the discussion. This is best since the long range interpersonal communication site highlight on a high convergence of a person's focused on gathering.

With regards to long range interpersonal communication site to advance locally established affiliate marketing organizations, it is urgent to guarantee that you are following the directions related with the social marketing destinations. The person to person communication locales now and again may have limitations with respect to the posting of connections and inability to keep the set confinements may influence you to be banned from the long range interpersonal communication destinations. Along these lines, any individual who is occupied with utilizing these destinations should peruse the client consent to guarantee that they are not damaging any standard.

Week by week, Or Monthly: Which Affiliate Pay Structure Is Best

When searching for an affiliate program that will be appropriate for your web venture it very well may be hard now and again. This is a result of the staggeringly many affiliate programs that are offered on the web. Above all else you ought to guarantee that the affiliate program is trustworthy and has become great outcomes for different organizations.

You have to inquire as to whether the program offers lingering profit. This sort of gain is got from income and is considered as installments issued month to month from each deal. If you discover an item that you are prepared to advance and it's from another dealer scan the web for comparable affiliate- sourced items. Realize what the program offers, and you keep on providing specific rates. This offers a person with great data of the deals that he or she will get for a specific decent.

Attempt and select a program that offers special assets since it is less complex to advance a thing if there are flags, locales and adverts that are given at no additionally cost. It can likewise make your advancement exercises more elegant and much less complex than you never anticipated. Consider the program that offers a decent pay structure; endeavor to get data concerning the manner in which the affiliate program performs. If you are even the littlest piece confounded, at that point you should shift to the program alternative. Affiliate projects ought to dependably be in a situation to make it right exactly how their specific program performs.

Try not to pick a program which will expect you to spend anything or necessities you to store a few items. As an affiliate, you turn out to be a piece of the partnership's deal constrain but you're utilized just on commission and ought not hold stock. Think of the leads for your affiliate by utilizing email bulletins. A web webpage is extremely vital for the most part when you are wanting to produce more money. Read up on an approach to construct a work-at-home business and what's required to make progress. This can sound an extremely basic point to you if this is your first time giving it a shot. Organize the components worried in affiliate programs. When you pursue basic advances, these inquiries can turn into significantly more straightforward to find solutions to, and finding the affiliate program appropriate for your web business will be simple.

Offer Your Prospects Bonus Incentives

What more often than not occurs when an affiliate advertiser goes to ClickBank or Commission Junction and joins as an affiliate advertiser for a specific item or administration that is in respect to his affiliate marketing business theme?

The main thing he does is typically to put a logo for the item on his site and convey a marketing email to his rundown upholding the estimation of whatever the item or administration happens to be. If this normal affiliate advertiser has any zip whatsoever, he will make his direct mail advertisement comparable to he can make it.

It will address every individual from his rundown by name and there will be visual cues posting the favorable circumstances furnished with responsibility for item or administration. At that point he will sit back, cross his fingers and toes, and want to make a couple of offers. Indeed, that IS an arrangement but is anything but a decent one.

If this normal affiliate advertiser happens to luck out and be incorporated into the dispatch of another item, he does essentially a similar thing. He notifies his rundown of the up and coming dispatch (the normal affiliate advertiser generally just sends one preliminary email) and afterward he conveys the marketing email at the dispatch.

He will make a couple of sales...very few. Obviously, he won't buckle down either and perhaps he is exceptionally upbeat being a normal affiliate advertiser. There is an issue, be that as it may, with being normal. Normal is an extremely swarmed place.

Normal! For what reason would anyone need to make due with normal anything? Doesn't 'normal' signify 'normal or ordinary...nothing unique'? If you are not content with being a normal affiliate advertiser, at that point you have to continue perusing.

What puts one affiliate advertiser over the normal affiliate advertiser? The appropriate response is uniqueness.

Being novel is a quality that separates one from every one of others. If you need to be superior to simply average, you should build up some uniqueness in your marketing methods that will set you above only a normal affiliate advertiser.

Normal affiliate advertisers simply don't get a handle on the possibility that with the end goal to offer a great deal of item, their offer should be more important than the offers their rivals are making. Most affiliate advertisers won't offer any motivators to their rundowns for purchasing a specific item from that point as opposed to purchasing a similar item from another person.

Some affiliate advertisers will offer some extra motivating forces but they will be truly conventional and things that are truly not of much esteem or even disconnected to the item that is being advanced.

The great affiliate advertiser will offer extra motivating forces that are BETTER than anything that is being offered by some other advertiser and are straightforwardly identified with the item that is being advanced. The great affiliate advertiser will give his clients a valid justification to purchase from him.

As a matter of fact, the entire thought of offering better motivators to clients is outright old presence of mind. If you can purchase 2 ears of corn from seller A for 20 pennies or 2 ears of corn from merchant B for 20 pennies and seller B tosses in some butter to go on the corn for nothing out of pocket, which seller would you say you will purchase from?

Affiliate marketing is the simple same thing.

You bring to the table rewards and you bring to the table preferred rewards over those that other affiliate advertisers are putting forth.

For instance: Let's say that there is an E-Book about Email Marketing than you are an affiliate advertiser for. It's a decent book that has been composed by an Email Marketing Guru. It is offering for $100 and your bonus will be $50 per deal that you make. There is an expound live dispatch for the item. Your rivals are putting forth an extra E-Book or two as extra motivations.

How might you get an edge here? The main way that you can get an edge is to offer something that your rivals are not advertising. You could have set up a free teleseminar that will happen inside a couple of days of the dispatch for the individuals who purchase from you or you could offer a free 30 minute downloadable sound tape that further clarifies certain focuses in the E-Book.

The general population who purchase from you will improve bargain than they could get from your rivals. The item will dependably be the same...but the rewards that are offered is the place you get the edge.

Tip: Never think little of the intensity of 'free'. Everyone adores getting something to no end or getting something additional. They particularly love getting something that every other person isn't getting. Also, that conveys me to another, better purpose of offering extra motivations.

If you can offer something, for example, a free teleseminar that is identified with an item dispatch, you have to constrain the quantity of individuals who will get the reward. That makes it more restrictive and in this way more attractive.

You would prefer not to make clients distraught but you would like to influence the individuals who to get the special rewards feel like they have gotten something others have not gotten. You may state your offer to state that the initial 200 individuals who purchase the item from you will be permitted to join the teleseminar live and others will get a transcript of the teleseminar. Like I stated, this is dubious but it very well may be finished.

The primary concern is only this: if you need to be a superior than normal affiliate advertiser you will bring to the table more and preferable extra motivations over your rivals offer. All affiliate advertisers for any item are on the whole endeavoring to pitch to a similar fundamental client base and that base isn't boundless.

With the end goal to get an edge and transcend what is normal, standard and normal you should get extremely innovative with the motivating force rewards that you offer with your affiliate item or administration.

Try not to Cut Yourself Short With Offering Rebates!

Discounts! Refunds appear to be extremely popular in the present commercial center. Discounts are all over the place. Out in the physical world there are 'mail-in' discounts and moment refunds offered on each item possible from PCs to home apparatuses to autos. In the internet the discount is all over the place. Refunds are offered on a wide range of projects, programming, items and administrations.

A refund is essentially a rebate in extravagant garments. The guideline is actually the equivalent. The client pays not as much as the rundown cost for whatever the program, programming, item or administration may be. The client is getting a deal. That is valid. The inquiry, nonetheless, is what precisely is the vender getting?

The response to the inquiry, what is the vender getting, is quite straightforward. The vender is getting less cash than he is qualified for get on each deal he makes.

If the dealer is giving a half refund that implies that he should offer double the quantity of projects, programming duplicates, items or administrations to make a similar measure of cash he would have made had he not offered the half discount.

The vender is giving ceaselessly his benefit particularly if the dealer is an affiliate advertiser in light of the fact that any refund an affiliate advertiser offers his clients leaves his bonus. For instance: if you are marketing an item that offers for $197.00 and you procure $98.50 from it, offering a discount of $50 implies that your bonus is just $48.50 per deal.

You wouldn't gain particularly per deal. That can't be something to be thankful for. There must be a superior route than offering huge rebates...and, luckily, there is.

One of the enormous issues with offering huge discounts is that the offer draws in what is referred to in the business as 'shoddy clients'. Shoddy clients are the individuals who never hope to pay the maximum for anything, ever or under any conditions. They hope to get something in vain and that something to no end desire will dependably leave your pocket. You are basically happier without modest clients.

The response to the discount question is only this: give your clients a valid justification to purchase from you at the maximum. Regardless of whether you need to pay something for impetus rewards, it is superior to offering a discount to the client.

You will pull in a superior class of clients who will keep on purchasing from you. Many affiliate advertisers imagine that offering motivator rewards that are sufficiently significant to lure individuals to pay the maximum for a thing is simply a lot of inconvenience. The clients that will be alluring by profound rebates and half refunds are the modest clients and once you markdown or offer a discount they will anticipate that you will do as such with each item or administration that you ever offer them. You will be working for peanuts when you could be working for the entire shelled nut display.

Try not to squander your time stressing over lethargic affiliate advertisers who offer profound rebates or enormous refunds. They will draw in the shoddy clients that you don't need at any rate and those languid affiliate advertisers will never be any opposition for you.

If you will go to the inconvenience, put in the work, and try to discover motivation rewards that make it feasible for you to pitch items at their the maximum to your clients, you will leave those sluggish affiliate advertisers eating your residue.

Before you much consider offering a refund or a markdown on an item or administration consider the reason that you turned into an affiliate advertiser in any case.

Did you turn into an affiliate advertiser with the goal that you could marginally scratch out a living or did you plan on making an exceptionally pleasant yearly wage that would give an extremely decent life style for you and your family? I question that scratching out a living was the best reason that you turned into an affiliate advertiser.

Take a gander at it like this: each time you acknowledge short of what you could get for an item, you are giving ceaselessly the lifestyle that you have been working for and you are agreeing to short of what you merit for yourself as well as for your family also.

It truly is never important to agree to less. It simply isn't important to offer an expansive refund or a profound markdown to offer a quality item or administration.

Individuals need, need and will pay for the items and administrations that they require. It isn't important to give away your benefit if you will simply work harder and discovering motivating force rewards that will lure your clients to purchase the items and administrations that they require from you.

Try not to markdown the item or offer a refund. Increment the estimation of the item. Keep in mind this; expanding esteem is superior to demeaning the item or administration that you are attempting to offer. Individuals don't generally observe a markdown or a discount as esteem. They now and again consider it to be an endeavor to lure them into purchasing an item that did not merit the maximum in any case.

Just the shabby clients will go for a refund or markdown. The great clients will look around to perceive what the best motivating forces being offered are. If you make your extra motivations the specific best, at that point you will pull in the best clients and you can charge the full approaching value each time and for each item or administration that you advance.

The most effective method to Win The Affiliate War

Winning the continuous affiliate war isn't simple but (in contrast to a few wars) it IS winnable. The affiliate wars can't and won't be won by sluggish affiliate advertisers. The affiliate marketing wars will be won by the forceful strategists who will buckle down and long.

Affiliate marketing isn't for the swoon of heart. If you had extremely known how intense the opposition is in affiliate marketing would you have joined the shred? It doesn't make a difference. You are amidst it now and stopping basically isn't a possibility for a genuine warrior. The main alternative is winning...and winning BIG!

Winning the affiliate marketing wars implies winning the little every day fights and minor clashes each one in turn and winning them conclusively.

You need to wind up one of those super affiliates. You need to end up one of those huge workers that make a yearly pay that has in excess of one comma in that number on the main issue, isn't that so?

At that point you should be set up to buckle down. You should be set up to accomplish more than what is required. You should be set up to go that additional mile.

Most importantly, notoriety checks in affiliate marketing. There are a huge number of affiliate advertisers out there but the ones who make gobs of cash are the ones who have set up high perceivability and extraordinary validity for themselves.

Building up believability and perceivability go as an inseparable unit and setting up both are basic to your prosperity and your triumph over your rivals.

Validity and perceivability are set up in a few different ways. Two of the most critical methods for setting up validity and perceivability are by composing and marketing articles and E-Books that identify with the items and administrations that you offer. You should build up yourself as an expert...a master, if you will.

You have to wind up the person or the lady that others go to when they require data or need questions replied. Composing articles and E-Books (or having them composed for you by a professional writer) is one of the specific most ideal methods for building up your notoriety for being a man who has answers.

Articles that you compose or have composed for you by a professional writer will be transferred into article banks for other site proprietors of E-zine distributers to download and recreate for nothing out of pocket. At the base of each 300-400 word, catchphrase rich article you will incorporate an asset box that has your name and your site address in it. This spreads your name and news of your insight around the Internet to the individuals who are the well on the way to be your clients.

Digital books should just be 10 to 12 pages in length but a connection to your site should be incorporated on each and every page and in addition in the asset box toward the end. digital books are transferred to E-Book storehouses where others may download them and replicate them simply like articles.

Since it is necessitated that E-Books can't be changed and that asset box data must be incorporated when E-Books are downloaded and duplicated, your notoriety for being a specialist in your field will be upgraded each time anybody utilizes them.

Another approach to manufacture your perceivability and your believability on the Internet is to post to websites and gatherings that have points identified with the items and administrations which you offer. It is an essentially matter to discover these gatherings and online journals. Essentially type your related catchphrase into the hunt box of your most loved web index pursued by the in addition to sign (+) and the words online journals or discussions. You will get numerous hits.

Pick the three or four of the ones that have the biggest number of dynamic individuals and join those websites or discussions. Be watchful here. Presenting on online journals and discussions adequately will take a few hours of your time each week so don't pick too much.

When you have joined three or four sites and discussions don't run in with weapons blasting posting glaring ads. The thought here is to assemble perceivability and believability. Present yourself and carry on as if you had quite recently moved into another area. Your mark label that shows up at the base of every single post that you make ought to have your name and additionally a connection to your site.

Set aside you opportunity to become acquainted with alternate blurbs in the network and turn into an esteemed individual from the gathering. You will assemble a decent notoriety, perceivability and believability.

It requires investment to assemble your perceivability and believability. While you are building them, you will likewise be advancing and offering items and administrations and you need to set up a decent association with the individuals who purchase items and administrations from you. Make sure that you give great data, great administration and a certification if one applies.

Put everything on the line to never give off an impression of being a cheapo or corner shaper to your clients. Continuously treat your clients like they are your most profitable asset...they ARE your most important resource.

Never markdown items or administrations or offer refunds. You would prefer not to assemble that sort of notoriety or that sort of client base. Rather than offering rebates or refunds take the time and set forth the push to add extra motivating forces to the items and administrations that you elevate to give them included esteem.

The champs of the affiliate wars are the people who go to the inconvenience and set aside the opportunity to construct amazing notorieties as specialists and as reasonable and legit vendors.

Individuals purchase things on the Internet from individuals that they have a feeling that they know and can trust. Individuals purchase things on the Internet from affiliate advertisers who have the notoriety for being a specialist or a master and one who really thinks about the general population to whom he pitches items and administrations to. A positive and persevering, fair– managing notoriety will enable you to win the day by day fights and, eventually the affiliate war.

Chapter 8

The Gift Package

12-Step video course on how to create your own online business with 'Private Label Rights' products

https://drive.google.com/open?id=1JgsKDmeiip8sQVESCrjsazuAyPPCv-IB

1,000 Ebooks with Private Label Rights

Part 1:
https://drive.google.com/file/d/1a1sDBfPMsDzi2HHh4QsefXRbKC5aCYtm/view?usp=sharing

Part 2:
https://drive.google.com/open?id=1mh8t56784UUGx9BXsy4sYElkQpKCajHt

Part 3:
https://drive.google.com/open?id=1jssbkZWzFssn9L0cWfkvybxy9R-CC8OB

Part 4:
https://drive.google.com/open?id=1W7bsgI7KUrN38efQky1hvXRt_93XRhZd

Part 5:
https://drive.google.com/open?id=11I3Q-UMyw6Hp6iQxpuCUfRvrZ8RuRR3r

Part 6:
https://drive.google.com/open?id=1uDJ5VonWYqRaUlu_bnbALltvlEdoYigS

Part 7:
https://drive.google.com/open?id=1RSVzCim4p8BcBRjGci856DZk5ASa_5M3

Part 8:
https://drive.google.com/open?id=1Uy2DCBnqcoGdXIuAtLSHDdhIKdA6IRjj

Part 9:
https://drive.google.com/open?id=18zHuM5lisggjrj7_ecyjcRti9zzrAeY5

Part 10:
https://drive.google.com/open?id=1IaGi1QkCnuegX4uiaWTVhk-wkhhUfVVJ

Part 11:
https://drive.google.com/open?id=1FNiBgH_HXcOYiVig6z2u9zOZyd4eA9uo

100,000 Articles with Private Label Rights

Part 1: https://drive.google.com/open?id=1X8XFj3FPDBGscf0GIPFGAHph2l3lW4me

Part 2: https://drive.google.com/open?id=1BV4UQdhIcQapeJiNSTKn9l0kN5B_czuT

How to download:

1. Type links in your web browser

2. Click download button (You may get this message "Google Drive can't scan this file for viruses". Ignore it and click 'Download Anyway' button. There are no any viruses in this package)

3. Once the Zip file is downloaded, right click and extract it to a folder you want

Shoot me an email and share your thoughts or ask any question: *brettsmith.kindle@gmail.com*

www.ingramcontent.com/pod-product-compliance
Lightning Source LLC
Chambersburg PA
CBHW071023240526
45469CB00006BD/2060